ideals

Wok COOKBOOK

By Carol DeMasters

Ideals Publishing Corp.

Milwaukee, Wisconsin

Contents

*Cover recipe: Shrimp and Vegetable Stir-Fry,
page 50*

ISBN 0-8249-3017-7

Copyright © MCMLXXXIII by Carol DeMasters
All rights reserved.
Printed and bound in the United States of America.
Published by Ideals Publishing Corporation
11315 Watertown Plank Road
Milwaukee, Wisconsin 53226
Published simultaneously in Canada

Wok Basics

Cooking in a wok is not difficult; it is different. You will acquire a feel for split-second timing, a sense of sequence and a knowledge of the amount of heat that will produce the best results. As you stir and toss food in the wok, your eyes will be on the food but your mind will be anticipating the next step.

Stir-frying is the most-used method of wok cookery. It is fast and fun, and results in delicious-tasting food. Searing meat and vegetables at high heat seals in their flavors, nutrients and juices while at the same time preserving their textures. A wonderful form of self-expression, stir-frying in a wok is a lot like tossing a salad. With a spatula in one hand and a ladle in the other, you maintain a constant motion of tossing and turning food over high heat.

Wok cookery need not necessarily mean Chinese cooking, although it is best illustrated in that ancient cuisine. Several of the recipes for basic, familiar foods in this book are not Chinese in origin. A wok can also be used in place of a conventional skillet, saucepan or deep-fryer. It can be a steamer when fitted with a rack or bamboo basket.

Wok cookery is adaptable. After you've made several stir-fry recipes in this book, you'll understand the technique, enabling you to combine your favorite foods in dishes which reflect your own personal style and taste preferences.

Using a wok, you will prepare nutritious, flavorful, crisp and colorful foods in a matter of minutes.

WOK COOKERY BASICS

Successful cooking in a wok depends on proper utensils and several cutting techniques and cooking methods.

UTENSILS

Chopsticks Wooden sticks that taper to points. They are used for stirring ingredients, beating eggs and testing oil temperature, in addition to being eating utensils. To determine if oil is hot enough for stir-frying, place one end of a chopstick into the oil. If the oil sizzles around the chopstick, it is hot enough to begin stir-frying.

Cleaver A broad, rectangular-bladed knife used for cutting, chopping, shredding, slicing and transferring food. A large chef's knife also may be used.

Ladle A metal utensil with a rounded scoop used for stir-frying foods to prevent them from burning.

Rack Made of wood or steel and used in a wok for steaming foods. The rack is placed over boiling water in a wok, and a plate or bowls of food may be set on it. The wok is covered so the food is steamed.

Ring Made of metal and placed on gas or electric burners to hold the wok steady during stir-frying. Place the ring with the smallest opening down on an electric burner. This will put the wok closer to the heat source. Reverse the ring on a gas burner. A ring also is a metal device which fits around the top circumference of a wok and is used as a place for tempura-fried foods to drain before serving.

Spatula A metal utensil used for stir-frying foods to prevent them from burning. It has a flatter scoop than the ladle.

Steamer Available in two forms. One is bamboo and can be set directly over boiling water in a wok and covered to steam or reheat foods. The other is an aluminum utensil that comes with manufacturer's directions for use in steaming and reheating foods.

Strainer A utensil with a shallow wire-net scoop and a bamboo or wooden handle. It is used to remove foods from hot oil or liquid in the wok.

Wok An all-purpose concave cooking pan with sloping sides that is thought to be one of the oldest cooking utensils. It cooks food evenly and quickly over very high heat. It is used for stir-frying, deep-frying, braising, stewing, blanching and steaming. Most woks are sold with a cover and ring. A 14-inch wok is standard, and most are made of steel, although they also can be stainless steel, copper, brass or aluminum. A rolled carbon steel wok must be seasoned so foods will not stick to it and so less oil can be used during stir-frying. To season a steel wok, first wash and dry it thoroughly. Put it over high heat and add ¼ cup cooking oil. Tilt the wok to coat its sides with oil. When the oil starts to smoke, remove the wok from the heat and let it cool. Wipe out the excess oil; repeat this process once more. Once seasoned, the wok should not be scrubbed with either an abrasive pad or cleanser. The best way to clean a wok is to soak it in warm water and use a sponge and mild detergent to remove any food particles. Dry the wok thoroughly and place it over high heat 30 seconds to prevent the formation of rust. Then lightly coat the inside of the wok with a small amount of cooking oil before storing it. Use and care of electric woks are best outlined by their manufacturer's directions.

Wok Basics

CUTTING TECHNIQUES

All ingredients for stir-frying in a wok should be cut in thin uniform-size pieces for attractive appearance and even, fast cooking. It is easier to cut meat in thin slices if it is partially frozen; then it will not slip under the pressure of a knife. Always slice across the grain to retain tenderness. Sharp knives are a must. Following are the cutting techniques used on most meats and vegetables:

1. **Slicing or Straight Cutting:** Hold the knife or cleaver straight up and down to cut to the desired thickness, usually from paper-thin to ½ inch thick.

2. **Shredding or Julienne Slicing:** Food is first sliced, then cut into uniform strips about the size of matchsticks. Shreds vary from ⅛ to ¼ inch thick and from 1½ to 2 inches long.

3. **Cubing:** Food is first sliced ½ inch thick, then again across the slices every ½ inch to produce ½-inch cubes.

4. **Chopping:** This is the coarsest cut and results in ½-inch pieces.

5. **Dicing:** Food is first sliced into thin slices, then into thin strips, then into small pieces varying from ¼ to ½ inch square.

6. **Mincing:** Food is chopped into rice-size pieces. It is much easier to mince vegetables if they are first chopped or diced.

7. **Diagonal Cutting:** Used mostly for vegetables. The knife or cleaver is held at a 45-degree angle for slicing. Practice with celery. Position the knife blade about ¾ inch from the end of the rib. Slant the knife blade away from you and slice the stalk with a sharp, angled cut. Discard this first irregular piece. Continue cutting at the same slant in small, regular intervals to produce thin, flat slices.

8. **Rolled or Oblique Cutting:** Used mostly for vegetables. The knife or cleaver is held at an angle to the food while the opposite hand rolls the food before the next cut is made, thus changing the angle of the cut. Practice with a carrot. Make a diagonal cut across the carrot; discard this first piece. Then, keeping the knife in the same position, roll the carrot over and cut through it diagonally again to form a piece with two slanted sides. Continue rolling and cutting in this manner.

COOKING METHODS

A wok is a versatile cooking utensil. All of the following cooking methods are possible in a wok.

Stir-Frying The most common cooking method in a wok, stir-frying is the vigorous stirring of food in a small amount of oil over high heat for a brief cooking time, usually just a few minutes. Before beginning, read the recipe through. Have all ingredients cut and/or measured as directed; place in small bowls arranged in the order in which they will be added to the wok. This can be done hours in advance. Have all utensils and serving pieces at easy access. Stir-frying should be done just before serving. Before beginning, reread the recipe. Stir-frying requires swift movements and split-second timing. Get used to the sound of sizzling, a sign of successful stir-frying. Heat the wok 30 seconds before adding the oil. Then drizzle soybean or peanut oil around the sides of the wok. Heat until hot. To test for hotness, flip a drop of water into the wok. If it sizzles and evaporates, the oil is hot enough. Then proceed as the recipe directs.

Deep-Frying Food cooks immersed in hot fat.

Blanching Food is parboiled in boiling water. When stir-frying, this is usually done to partially cook vegetables before they are completely cooked in the wok. They are immersed in boiling water, partially cooked and rinsed in cold water to stop the cooking and to set bright color.

Braising Food cooks in a small amount of liquid in a covered wok on low heat.

Steaming This method uses no oil. It can be done on a rack or in a bamboo basket in a wok. To steam food, place the rack above 2 to 3 inches of water in a wok. The rack and the food should not touch the water. Bring the water to a rapid boil, place the food on a shallow heatproof plate and place the plate on the rack. Cover the wok. If using a bamboo basket, place the food in it, cover the basket with the bamboo lid and place over boiling water. It is not necessary to cover the wok.

Simmering Food cooks at temperatures low enough to cause bubbles to appear and barely break the surface of the cooking liquid.

Appetizers

Chicken Nuggets in Spinach with Oriental Dip

Makes 30 pieces
Preparation Time: 45 minutes

> 1 whole chicken breast, split, boned and skinned
> 1¾ cups chicken stock
> ¼ cup soy sauce
> 1 tablespoon Worcestershire sauce
> 1 bunch fresh spinach, washed, stems discarded
> Oriental Dip

Simmer chicken breasts in chicken stock, soy sauce and Worcestershire sauce in wok until tender, 15 to 20 minutes. Remove from liquid; cool. Discard liquid. Pour 1 quart boiling water over spinach in colander; drain; set aside to cool. When chicken is cool enough to handle, cut into 30 bite-size pieces. Place 1 chicken piece at stem end of 1 spinach leaf, top side facing counter. Roll over once, folding leaf in on both sides; continue rolling around chicken piece. Place seam-side-down on decorative platter. Place dip in small bowl in center of platter. Spear each chicken piece with toothpick.

Note: Wrapped chicken can be prepared ahead of time, wrapped in plastic wrap and refrigerated. Dip can also be made in advance.

Oriental Dip

> 1 cup sour cream
> 2 teaspoons toasted sesame seed
> ½ teaspoon ground ginger
> 4 teaspoons soy sauce
> 2 teaspoons Worcestershire sauce

Mix all ingredients in bowl; chill at least 4 hours.

Chinese-Flavored Beef

Makes approximately 40 pieces
Preparation Time: 15 minutes; 1 hour to cook

> 2 tablespoons peanut oil
> 4 green onions, cut in 1-inch pieces
> 1 tablespoon peeled and minced fresh gingerroot
> 1 pound boneless beef chuck, cut in 1-inch cubes
> Sauce Mixture

Heat oil in wok until hot. Add onions and gingerroot; stir-fry 1 minute. Add beef cubes; stir-fry 2 to 3 minutes or until browned. Add Sauce Mixture; reduce heat to simmer; cover; cook 30 minutes. Uncover; increase heat to high; cook until sauce

thickens, about 30 minutes. Remove from wok; serve hot with picks for spearing meat.

Sauce Mixture

> ¼ cup sugar
> 2 tablespoons soy sauce
> ⅓ cup dry sherry
> 1 cup water
> ½ teaspoon dried red pepper flakes

Mix all ingredients until sugar dissolves.

Crab Won Tons

Makes 36
Preparation Time: 30 minutes

> 1 8-ounce package cream cheese, softened
> 1 6-ounce package frozen crab meat, thawed and drained
> 36 won ton skins
> Peanut oil
> Sweet and Sour Sauce (Recipe on page 31)

Mix cream cheese and crab meat in bowl. Place 1 teaspoon in middle of won ton skin; moisten edges with cold water; fold to form triangle; seal edges by pressing together. Prepare remaining won tons in same manner. Heat 2 inches oil in wok until hot. Fry won tons on both sides until golden. Drain on paper towels; keep warm. Serve with Sweet and Sour Sauce for dipping.

Curry Won Tons

Makes 20
Preparation Time: 20 minutes

> 1 8-ounce package cream cheese
> 20 won ton skins
> ⅓ cup chopped green onion
> Curry powder
> Peanut oil

Cut cream cheese into 20 equal pieces. Place 1 cheese cube in center of each won ton skin. Top with some green onion; sprinkle with curry powder. Moisten edges of won ton skins with cold water; fold to form triangle, sealing edges. Heat 2 inches oil in wok until hot. Fry won tons until golden. Drain on paper towels. Serve immediately.

Shrimp Toast

Makes approximately 32 pieces
Preparation Time: 20 minutes; 10 minutes to cook

      1 6-ounce can shrimp, drained and minced
      3 ounces ground lean pork
   1½ teaspoons dry sherry
   1½ teaspoons soy sauce
      ½ teaspoon salt
      ¼ teaspoon freshly ground black pepper
      ¼ cup finely chopped green onions
      ¾ teaspoon cornstarch
      ½ teaspoon sesame oil
      2 eggs
      7 to 8 slices thin white bread
      ⅓ cup fine dry bread crumbs
      1 cup peanut oil

Mix shrimp with next 8 ingredients and 1 egg. Spread shrimp mixture generously over 1 side of each slice of bread. Beat remaining egg in bowl; brush over bread and filling. Sprinkle bread crumbs over filling. Cut bread diagonally into quarters. Heat oil in wok over high heat until hot. Slide bread triangles, a few at a time, filling-side-down, into hot oil. Fry until golden; turn to brown other side. Drain on paper towels. Serve hot.

Note: Shrimp Toast can be made 30 minutes in advance; keep warm in 200° oven.

Chinese Pancakes

Makes 8
Preparation Time: 30 minutes

      1 cup flour
      ½ cup boiling water
      2 tablespoons sesame oil

Stir flour and water in bowl until flour comes away from sides of bowl. Knead on lightly floured board until smooth. Cover; let rest 20 minutes. Knead 1 minute; shape into 1½-inch diameter roll. Cut into 8 equal pieces. Flatten each to thin round pancake. Brush 1 side of each pancake with sesame oil; place 2 pancakes together, oiled sides touching. Roll each to 7-inch circle. Heat griddle; cook pancake on both sides until slightly puffy. Do not brown. Remove; separate 2 pancakes. Store between sheets of foil; wrap entire stack in foil. Place foil packet on rack or in bamboo steamer in wok. Add hot water to within ½-inch of rack or basket. Bring water to boil; cover; steam 10 minutes. For extra flavor, spread pancakes with Duck Sauce before filling. Serve with Mo Shu Pork or any shredded meat or vegetable stir-fry.

Note: Pancakes can be prepared in advance. Re-steam before serving. Pancakes can be frozen. Thaw in foil; steam 20 minutes.

Fried Walnuts

Makes approximately 4 cups
Preparation Time: 5 minutes; overnight to marinate; 10 to 15 minutes to cook

      1 cup water
      ¾ cup sugar
      1 pound walnut halves
         Peanut oil

Combine water and sugar in saucepan; cook 5 minutes to make syrup. Place walnuts in jar with cover; top with syrup. Cool; cover; let stand overnight; drain. Heat oil in wok until hot. Add nuts in batches; fry 2 to 3 minutes. Remove from oil with strainer. Drain on paper towels. Serve immediately.

Gingered Pork Balls

Makes 12 to 16
Preparation Time: 20 minutes

      1 pound ground pork
      1 cup coarsely chopped water chestnuts
      ½ teaspoon peeled and chopped fresh gingerroot
      1 egg, lightly beaten
      1 tablespoon soy sauce
         Cornstarch
         Peanut oil

Mix first 5 ingredients lightly. Shape into bite-size balls; roll lightly in cornstarch. Heat 2 inches oil in wok until hot. Add pork balls, a few at a time; fry until golden brown and cooked through. Drain on paper towels; serve hot with wooden picks.

Nacho Won Tons

Makes 20
Preparation Time: 20 minutes

      6 ounces sharp Cheddar cheese, shredded
   20 won ton skins
      1 4-ounce can chopped mild *or* hot green chilies, drained
         Peanut oil

Dividing cheese equally, place in middle of each won ton skin. Top each with ¼ teaspoon chilies. Moisten edges of won ton skins with cold water; fold to form triangle, sealing edges. Heat 2 inches oil in wok until hot. Fry won tons on both sides until browned. Drain on paper towels. Serve immediately.

Oriental Spareribs

Makes approximately 2 dozen
Preparation Time: 1½ hours

    2 cups water
    ½ cup soy sauce
    1 clove garlic, peeled and minced
    3 pounds spareribs, cut in 2-inch pieces
    2 tablespoons packed light brown sugar
    1 tablespoon cornstarch
    1 tablespoon sesame seed
    2 tablespoons chopped green onion
    1 ¼-inch slice fresh gingerroot, peeled and minced

Mix water, ¼ cup soy sauce and garlic in wok. Add spareribs; bring to boil. Reduce heat; cover; simmer on low heat 1 hour. Remove cover; bring to boil; cook 20 minutes. Drain; reserve ¼ cup cooking liquid. Mix remaining ¼ cup soy sauce and remaining ingredients. Place spareribs and reserved ¼ cup cooking liquid in wok over medium heat. Pour seasoned soy sauce over ribs; cook, spooning sauce over ribs until it thickens and adheres to ribs, about 10 minutes. Serve warm.

Note: These can be made 3 to 4 hours in advance; reheat in microwave oven or in conventional 350° oven 10 minutes.

Egg Rolls

Makes 4 to 5 dozen
Preparation Time: 1 hour

    2 tablespoons peanut oil
    3 ribs celery, cut in 1-inch julienne pieces
    6 green onions, cut in 1-inch julienne pieces
    ¾ teaspoon salt
    ¾ teaspoon sugar
    1½ pounds finely chopped lean pork *or* chicken *or* shrimp
    1 8-ounce can sliced bamboo shoots, drained and coarsely chopped
    2 cups fresh bean sprouts
    2 tablespoons soy sauce
    2 tablespoons dry sherry
    1 1-pound package egg roll skins
    1 egg white, lightly beaten
    Peanut oil
    Sweet and Sour Sauce (Recipe on page 31) *or* Hot Mustard Sauce (Recipe on page 31) *or* Duck Sauce

Heat 1 tablespoon oil in wok until hot. Add next 4 ingredients; stir-fry 2 minutes. Remove to large bowl; set aside. Heat 1½ teaspoons oil in wok until hot; add pork and bamboo shoots; stir-fry 1 minute. Remove to bowl. Heat remaining 1½ teaspoons oil in wok until hot; add bean sprouts;

stir-fry 2 minutes; remove to bowl. Stir soy sauce and sherry into mixture in bowl. Place in strainer to drain thoroughly, at least 10 minutes. Place 1 egg roll skin on counter with a corner toward you. Put 1 tablespoon filling in rectangular mound on center of wrapper. Fold bottom corner of wrapper up over filling; overlap 2 opposite side corners. Moisten 4th or top corner with egg white; fold over to form roll. Heat 2 inches oil in wok until hot. Fry egg rolls, two to three at a time, until golden brown. Drain on paper towels. Serve with sauce of your choice.

Note: After frying, egg rolls can be covered and refrigerated no longer than 24 hours. Heat, uncovered, in 350° oven about 15 minutes or until heated through.

Fried Won Tons

Makes approximately 50
Preparation Time: 30 minutes; 10 minutes to cook

    ¼ pound ground lean pork *or* chicken *or* beef
    1 6-ounce can shrimp, drained and minced
    ¼ cup minced mushrooms
    ¼ cup diced water chestnuts
    1 green onion, finely chopped
    2 egg yolks
    1 tablespoon soy sauce
    1½ teaspoons peanut oil
    ¾ pound won ton skins (about 50)
    Peanut oil
    Won Ton Sauce

Mix first 8 ingredients in wok over medium heat. Cook, stirring often, about 5 minutes. Cool. Place about 1 tablespoon mixture in middle of each won ton skin. Moisten edges of wrapper with cold water; fold in half diagonally to form triangle; press edges together to seal. Fry won tons in hot oil in wok until golden on both sides; drain on paper towels. Serve with sauce.

Note: Can be prepared 1 hour in advance; keep warm in 200° oven.

Won Ton Sauce

    2 tablespoons cornstarch
    3 tablespoons light brown sugar, packed
    ¼ cup soy sauce
    ¾ cup water
    1 clove garlic, peeled and sliced
    1 tablespoon peanut oil

Stir first 4 ingredients until smooth. Fry garlic in hot oil in wok on low heat until light brown. Remove garlic; set aside. Slowly pour cornstarch mixture into hot oil; cook, stirring, until thickened. Top with fried garlic.

Fried Won Tons, this page;
Egg Rolls, this page

Soups

Chinese Cucumber Soup

Makes 6 to 8 servings
Preparation Time: 30 minutes

- 1 tablespoon dry sherry
- 2 tablespoons soy sauce
- 1 tablespoon cornstarch
- ½ pound boned and skinned chicken breast *or* finely shredded lean pork
- 2 tablespoons peanut oil
- 6 cups chicken stock
- 2 green onions, thinly sliced
- 1 medium cucumber, peeled, split lengthwise, seeds removed, diced
- 1½ teaspoons salt
- ¼ teaspoon freshly ground white pepper
- 1 egg, lightly beaten

Mix first 3 ingredients in bowl; add chicken; stir to coat. Heat oil in wok over high heat. Add chicken; stir-fry 3 to 5 minutes. Add chicken stock; reduce heat; simmer 10 to 12 minutes. Add next 4 ingredients; simmer 5 minutes. Increase heat; bring soup to fast boil; remove from heat; stir in egg. Serve immediately.

Egg Drop Soup with Shrimp

Makes 6 to 8 servings
Preparation Time: 20 minutes

- 6 cups chicken stock
  Salt and freshly ground white pepper to taste
  Pinch cayenne pepper
- ½ cup frozen peas
- 16 medium shrimp, shelled and deveined
- 2 tablespoons cornstarch mixed with
  ¼ cup cold water
- 2 eggs, lightly beaten with 1 teaspoon soy sauce
- 2 green onions, thinly sliced

Heat chicken stock, salt, pepper and cayenne pepper in wok over high heat to just under a boil. Add peas; cook 1 minute. Add shrimp; cook until pink. Add cornstarch mixture, stirring until slightly thickened. Remove from heat; swirl in eggs using fork. Garnish with onions; serve immediately.

Hot and Sour Soup

Makes 4 to 6 servings
Preparation Time: 25 minutes; 20 minutes to cook

- 4 cups chicken stock
- 6 ounces lean pork *or* chicken breast, cut in julienne strips
- ½ cup tofu, cut in julienne strips
- ½ cup bamboo shoots, cut in julienne strips
- 6 cloud ear mushrooms, soaked in ½ cup hot water 15 minutes, stems discarded, caps halved
- 6 Chinese dried black mushrooms, soaked in ½ cup hot water 15 minutes, stems discarded, caps thinly sliced
- 1 tablespoon soy sauce
- ¼ teaspoon sugar
- ¾ teaspoon salt
- 2 tablespoons cornstarch mixed with 3 tablespoons water
- 1 egg, beaten until slightly foamy
- 3 tablespoons Chinese red vinegar
- ½ teaspoon ground white pepper
- 2 green onions including tops, thinly sliced

Bring chicken stock to boil in wok over high heat. Add pork, tofu, bamboo shoots, cloud ear and Chinese mushrooms; cook 3 to 5 minutes. Mix soy sauce, sugar, salt and cornstarch mixture; add to soup; stir; cook until soup just comes to a boil. Slowly swirl in egg; remove from heat immediately. Put vinegar and pepper in bowl; add soup and green onions. Stir; serve immediately.

Hot Oriental Mushroom Soup

Makes 4 to 6 servings
Preparation Time: 30 minutes

- 4 cups chicken stock
- 6 Chinese dried black mushrooms, soaked in hot water 20 minutes, drained, stems discarded, caps thinly sliced
- ¼ cup Madeira
  Chopped green onion

Bring stock to boil in wok over high heat. Add mushrooms and wine; reduce heat and cover; simmer 20 minutes. Sprinkle with green onion; serve immediately.

Japanese Soup

Makes 6 to 8 servings
Preparation Time: 25 minutes

- **6 cups chicken stock**
- **¼ cup dry sherry**
- **1½ tablespoons soy sauce**
- **6 to 8 fresh mushrooms, wiped clean and thinly sliced**
- **1 teaspoon lemon juice**
- **6 green onions, cut in ½-inch diagonal slices**
- **1 small carrot, pared and cut in thin diagonal slices**
- **¼ pound tiny shelled shrimp, optional**

Bring stock to simmer in wok over high heat. Stir in sherry and soy sauce; simmer 5 minutes. Add remaining ingredients; bring to boil; simmer 5 minutes. Serve immediately.

Noodles and Vegetables in Broth

Makes 6 servings.
Preparation Time: 20 minutes

- **8 ounces wide egg noodles**
- **6 cups chicken stock**
- **2 cups cubed cooked chicken, turkey, pork or ham**
- **1 carrot, pared and cut in thin diagonal slices**
- **1 large rib celery, cut in thin diagonal slices**
- **2 green onions, halved lengthwise and cut diagonally in 1-inch pieces**
- **½ cup thinly sliced bok choy (Chinese cabbage)**
- **2 tablespoons soy sauce**
- **Salt and freshly ground white pepper to taste**

Cook noodles according to package directions; drain; rinse under cold running water to stop cooking; set aside. Heat chicken stock in wok over high heat. Add next 6 ingredients; season to taste with salt and pepper. Simmer 5 to 10 minutes to just barely cook vegetables. Divide noodles among 6 soup bowls; ladle in soup. Serve immediately.

Oriental Spring Soup

Makes 6 servings
Preparation Time: 10 minutes; 15 minutes to cook

- **5 cups chicken stock**
- **½ cup julienne-cut carrot**
- **½ cup peas, fresh or frozen**
- **½ cup fresh spinach leaves, washed, stems discarded, shredded**
- **¼ cup finely sliced green onion**
- **2 tablespoons minced fresh parsley**
- **Salt and freshly ground white pepper to taste**

Bring chicken stock to simmer in wok over high heat. Add carrot and peas; cook 5 minutes. Add spinach, green onion and parsley; simmer 2 minutes. Add salt and pepper to taste. Serve immediately.

Spinach Soup with Pork Balls

Makes 4 servings
Preparation Time: 1 hour

- **6 cups chicken stock**
- **2 ¼-inch peeled slices fresh gingerroot**
- **4 Chinese dried black mushrooms, soaked in hot water 20 minutes, drained, stems discarded, caps thinly sliced**
- **Salt and freshly ground white pepper to taste**
- **2 green onions, minced**
- **¼ cup minced water chestnuts**
- **½ pound lean ground pork**
- **1 tablespoon soy sauce**
- **1 teaspoon dry sherry**
- **2 teaspoons cornstarch**
- **½ cup loosely packed spinach leaves, washed, stems discarded, shredded**

Bring chicken stock and 2 slices gingerroot to simmer in wok over high heat. Add mushrooms, salt and pepper; simmer 15 minutes. Remove gingerroot. Mix next 6 ingredients; form into 12 1¼-inch balls. Add pork balls to stock; simmer 30 minutes or until cooked through. Add spinach 3 minutes before serving; serve immediately.

Velvet Corn Soup

Makes 6 to 8 servings
Preparation Time: 10 minutes; 15 minutes to cook

- **6 cups hot chicken stock**
- **2 tablespoons cornstarch**
- **1 tablespoon peanut oil**
- **4 green onions, white part only, minced**
- **2 cups cream-style corn, pureed in food processor or blender**
- **¼ teaspoon salt**
- **¼ teaspoon freshly ground white pepper**
- **1 tablespoon dry sherry**
- **2 egg whites, lightly beaten until frothy**
- **2 tablespoons minced cooked ham**

Pour ¼ cup chicken stock over cornstarch in small bowl; stir to combine; set aside. Heat oil in wok over high heat. Add onions; stir-fry 30 to 45 seconds. Add remaining stock, corn, salt, pepper and sherry; simmer 15 minutes over medium heat. Increase heat; bring soup to boil; add cornstarch mixture. Stir until soup is slightly thickened, about 3 minutes. Remove from heat; add egg whites; stir to combine. Stir in ham; serve immediately.

Watercress Soup with Ham Shreds

Makes 6 to 8 servings
Preparation Time: 30 minutes

    8 cups chicken stock
    ½ teaspoon five-spice powder
    2 teaspoons salt
    1 teaspoon sugar
    2 tablespoons dry sherry
    2 ¼-inch slices fresh gingerroot, peeled
    4 green onions, sliced
    2 bunches watercress, washed, stems discarded
    ½ cup thinly sliced ham

Put first 7 ingredients in wok over high heat; bring to boil; cook 10 minutes; strain, reserving stock. Return stock to wok over high heat; bring to boil; add watercress and ham; return to boil. Serve immediately.

Won Ton Soup

Makes 6 servings plus leftover won tons
Preparation Time: 1 hour; 10 minutes to cook

    6 Chinese dried black mushrooms, soaked in hot water 20 minutes, drained, stems discarded, caps minced
    ¼ pound ground lean pork
    ¼ pound shrimp, coarsely chopped
    3 teaspoons minced green onion
    2 tablespoons soy sauce
    ½ teaspoon salt
    1 teaspoon sesame oil
       Dash freshly ground white pepper
    1 pound won ton skins
    1 egg white, lightly beaten
    6 cups hot chicken stock
       Finely sliced green onions, optional

Mix first 8 ingredients. Place ½ teaspoon filling in center of each won ton skin. Moisten edges with egg white; fold in triangle; press edges to seal. Moisten the two far points of triangle with water; press together firmly. Makes about 55 won tons. Drop 18 won tons into wok of boiling water; cook 10 minutes; drain. Place 3 won tons in each of 6 soup bowls; fill with hot chicken stock; garnish with green onions, if desired. Serve immediately.

Note: Remaining won tons can be frozen. It is not necessary to thaw before cooking.

Far East Tofu Soup

Makes 4 to 6 servings
Preparation Time: 20 minutes; 30 minutes to cook

    2 tablespoons peanut oil
    1½ cups sliced fresh mushrooms
    3 large cloves garlic, peeled and crushed
    ½ teaspoon peeled and minced fresh gingerroot
    3 tablespoons soy sauce
    2½ cups chicken stock
    1½ cups water
    1 cup uncooked egg noodles
    1 unpeeled medium zucchini, cut in ½-inch pieces
    1 cup cleaned and finely chopped fresh spinach
    ¼ pound tofu, cut in ½-inch cubes
    ⅓ cup finely chopped green onions including tops

Heat oil in wok over high heat. Add next 3 ingredients; stir-fry 2 minutes. Add soy sauce; take off heat. Bring stock and water to boil in another wok over high heat; add noodles; boil 2 minutes; reduce heat to simmer; add zucchini and spinach; simmer 6 to 8 minutes. Add tofu and reserved mushroom mixture; simmer 8 to 10 minutes. Garnish with green onions. Serve immediately.

Zucchini and Pasta Soup

Makes 4 servings
Preparation Time: 15 minutes; 12 minutes to cook

    ¼ cup olive oil
    1 medium onion, peeled and chopped
    1 clove garlic, peeled and crushed
    4 unpeeled medium zucchini, cut in 1½-inch-long julienne strips
    1 tomato, peeled, seeded and chopped
    ½ teaspoon basil
       Salt and freshly ground white pepper to taste
    3 cups chicken stock
    2 cups cold cooked pasta (such as macaroni, small shells *or* bow knots)

Heat oil in wok until hot. Stir-fry onion and garlic 30 seconds. Add next 5 ingredients; cover; simmer 10 minutes. Stir in pasta; heat thoroughly. Serve immediately.

Clockwise, from top:
Won Ton Soup, this page;
Japanese Soup, page 13;
Egg Drop Soup with Shrimp, page 12

Tofu

Tofu with Oyster Sauce

Makes 4 servings
Preparation Time: 5 minutes; 4 minutes to cook

　2 tablespoons peanut oil
　½ teaspoon minced garlic
　2 green onions, thinly sliced
　½ pound tofu, cut in ½-inch cubes
　½ cup chicken stock
　2 tablespoons oyster sauce
　1 teaspoon cornstarch mixed with
　　2 teaspoons cold water

Heat oil in wok until hot. Add garlic and green onions; stir-fry 30 seconds. Add tofu; gently stir-fry 1 minute. Add stock and oyster sauce; cover; cook 1 minute. Uncover; stir cornstarch mixture; add to wok; stir until slightly thickened. Serve immediately.

Fried Tofu

Makes 4 servings
Preparation Time: 20 minutes

　1 pound tofu
　¼ teaspoon salt
　3 eggs, lightly beaten
　¼ cup flour
　2 tablespoons water
　　Peanut oil
　¼ teaspoon crushed fresh gingerroot
　1 green onion including top, finely chopped
　1 tablespoon soy sauce

Cut tofu in half horizontally; sprinkle with salt; let stand 10 minutes. Pat dry; cut tofu in 1 x 2-inch pieces. Mix next 3 ingredients in bowl until smooth. Heat 1 tablespoon oil in wok until hot. Dip tofu pieces, one at a time, in batter; fry, three to four at a time, in oil until golden brown. (Add more oil if necessary.) Heat 2 tablespoons oil in wok. Add gingerroot and green onion; stir-fry 10 seconds. Return tofu to wok with soy sauce; cover; cook 1 minute. Serve immediately.

Scrambled Tofu

Makes 4 servings
Preparation Time: 5 minutes; 4 minutes to cook

　1½ tablespoons peanut oil
　1 pound tofu, cut in ½-inch cubes
　　Juice of ½ lemon
　　Salt and freshly ground black pepper to taste
　1 medium onion, peeled, halved, and thinly sliced
　½ pound snow peas, ends and strings removed
　½ teaspoon dried thyme

Heat oil in wok until hot. Add tofu; gently stir-fry 2 minutes. Add remaining ingredients; stir-fry 2 minutes. Serve immediately.

Spicy Tofu

Makes 4 servings
Preparation Time: 5 minutes; 4 minutes to cook

　3 tablespoons hot bean paste
　1 tablespoon dry sherry
　1 teaspoon sesame oil
　2 tablespoons peanut oil
　1 teaspoon salt
　2 onions, peeled, halved and thinly sliced
　1 pound tofu, cut in ½-inch cubes

Mix first 3 ingredients; set aside. Heat oil in wok until hot. Add salt and onions; stir-fry 2 minutes. Add tofu; gently stir-fry 1 minute. Add bean paste mixture; stir-fry to coat. Serve immediately.

Stir-Fried Tofu and Vegetables

Makes 4 servings
Preparation Time: 10 minutes; 5 minutes to cook

　2 tablespoons peanut oil
　1 clove garlic, peeled and crushed
　¼ pound fresh mushrooms, wiped clean and thinly sliced
　1 carrot, pared and cut in thin diagonal slices
　1 onion, peeled, halved and thinly sliced
　1 green pepper, cored, seeded and cut in ½-inch pieces
　3 tablespoons soy sauce
　½ teaspoon sugar
　1 pound tofu, cut in ½-inch cubes
　1 teaspoon cornstarch mixed with
　　2 teaspoons cold water

Heat oil in wok until hot. Add garlic and mushrooms; stir-fry 30 seconds. Add next 3 ingredients; stir-fry 2 minutes. Add soy sauce, sugar and tofu; stir-fry 10 seconds. Cover; cook 1 minute. Uncover; stir cornstarch mixture; add to wok. Stir-fry until slightly thickened. Serve immediately.

Flavored Rice

Makes 4 servings
Preparation Time: 10 minutes; 5 minutes to cook

> 1 tablespoon sesame oil
> 3 tablespoons toasted sesame seed
> 3 green onions, minced
> 2 cloves garlic, peeled and crushed
> 1½ cups fresh bean sprouts
> 2 cups hot cooked rice
> 2 tablespoons soy sauce

Heat oil in wok until hot. Add next 3 ingredients; stir-fry until onions soften, about 1 minute. Add bean sprouts; stir-fry until heated through. Add rice and soy sauce; toss to combine. Heat through. Serve immediately.

Pork Fried Rice

Makes 4 servings
Preparation Time: 15 minutes; 7 minutes to cook

> 2 tablespoons peanut oil
> ½ pound lean pork, cut in thin strips
> ½ teaspoon sugar
> ½ teaspoon salt
> ½ cup thinly sliced green onions including tops
> ½ cup thinly sliced celery
> 2 cups cold cooked rice
> 1 cup fresh bean sprouts
> 3 tablespoons soy sauce
> 3 eggs, lightly beaten

Heat oil in wok until hot. Add next 3 ingredients; stir-fry 2 to 3 minutes. Add green onions and celery; stir-fry 1 minute. Add rice and bean sprouts; stir-fry 30 seconds. Add soy sauce; stir to mix. Make well in center of rice; pour in beaten eggs; allow to set; scramble with spatula; stir into rice. Serve immediately.

Vegetarian Fried Rice

Makes 4 to 6 servings
Preparation Time: 10 minutes; 5 minutes to cook

> 2 tablespoons peanut oil
> ½ teaspoon salt
> 2 eggs, lightly beaten
> ⅔ cup thinly sliced green onions
> 1 cup fresh bean sprouts
> 3 tablespoons soy sauce
> 3 cups cold cooked rice
>   Freshly ground black pepper to taste

Heat oil in wok until hot. Add salt and eggs; scramble quickly, breaking into small pieces with

spatula. Add onions; stir-fry 2 minutes. Add bean sprouts; stir-fry 1 minute. Add soy sauce, rice and pepper; stir-fry until heated through, about 1 minute. Serve immediately.

Stir-Fried Noodles

Makes 4 servings
Preparation Time: 20 minutes; 2 to 3 minutes to cook

> 3 tablespoons peanut oil
> 1 1-inch piece fresh gingerroot, peeled and finely chopped
> 6 Chinese dried black mushrooms, soaked in hot water 20 minutes, drained, stems discarded, caps thinly sliced
> 3 green onions, thinly sliced
> ½ teaspoon salt
> 8 ounces Chinese noodles, cooked and drained
> 2 tablespoons soy sauce
> 1 teaspoon sesame oil
> 1 tablespoon dry sherry

Heat oil in wok until hot. Add next 4 ingredients; stir-fry 30 seconds. Add remaining ingredients; stir-fry to combine and heat. Serve immediately.

Subgum Fried Rice

Makes 4 servings
Preparation Time: 15 minutes; 5 minutes to cook

> 2 tablespoons peanut oil
> ¼ cup thinly sliced green onions including tops
> ¼ cup frozen peas
> ¼ cup diced cooked shrimp
> ¼ cup diced cooked lean ham
> 2 eggs, lightly beaten
> ½ teaspoon salt
> 2 cups cold cooked rice
> 2 tablespoons soy sauce

Heat oil in wok until hot. Add onions; stir-fry 30 seconds. Add next 3 ingredients; stir-fry 1 minute. Push to one side of wok; add eggs; sprinkle with salt; scramble; cut apart with spatula; mix in with other ingredients. Add rice and soy sauce; stir-fry to mix and heat through, about 2 minutes. Serve immediately.

Rice and Noodles

Spicy Noodles and Ham

Makes 6 servings
Preparation Time: 5 minutes; 2 minutes to cook

- 1½ quarts water
- ½ teaspoon salt
- 1 pound Chinese egg noodles
- 1 teaspoon sesame oil
- 3 tablespoons soy sauce
- 1½ tablespoons vinegar
- 1 teaspoon sugar
- ½ teaspoon hot pepper sauce
- 3 tablespoons chopped green onion
- ½ cup chicken stock
- 1 cup shredded cooked ham

Bring water and salt to boil in wok. Add noodles; boil 2 minutes, stirring constantly. Drain; rinse under cold running water to stop cooking. Drain; pour into bowl; stir in sesame oil. Mix next 6 ingredients; pour over noodles; toss to combine. Add ham; toss. Serve cold or at room temperature.

Fried Rice with Ham

Makes 4 servings
Preparation Time: 15 minutes; 5 minutes to cook

- 2 tablespoons peanut oil
- ⅓ cup thinly sliced green onions including tops
- ½ teaspoon peeled and minced fresh gingerroot
- ½ teaspoon minced garlic
- 2 eggs, lightly beaten
- ¼ teaspoon salt
- ¼ teaspoon sugar
- ⅓ pound finely diced cooked lean ham
- ½ cup frozen tiny peas
- 2 tablespoons soy sauce
- 2 cups cold cooked rice
- ½ teaspoon sesame oil

Heat oil in wok until hot. Add next 3 ingredients; stir-fry 1 minute. Add eggs; scramble loosely; break up with spatula. Add next 5 ingredients; stir-fry 2 minutes. Add rice; stir-fry 30 seconds. Add sesame oil; stir and serve immediately.

Note: Leftover fried rice can be refrigerated and reheated as well as frozen, thawed and reheated. For best results with fried rice recipes, be sure rice is cold before stir-frying.

Red Pepper Rice

Makes 4 servings
Preparation Time: 20 minutes; 20 minutes to cook

- 3 tablespoons olive oil
- 4 cloves garlic, peeled, split lengthwise
- 2 onions, peeled and chopped
  Pinch dried red pepper flakes
- 1 cup long-grain rice
- ½ small red pepper, cored, seeded and diced
- 1 small tomato, cored, peeled and chopped
- 1½ cups chicken stock
  Salt to taste

Heat oil in wok until hot. Add garlic; swirl around in hot oil 30 seconds; remove and discard. Add onions; stir-fry 1 minute. Add pepper flakes; stir-fry 10 seconds. Add rice; stir-fry 2 to 3 minutes or until all grains are coated with oil. Add next 3 ingredients; stir and bring to boil. Cover; reduce heat and simmer 15 minutes. Fluff rice with fork; season with salt. Serve immediately.

Noodle Salad with Oriental Dressing

Makes 4 servings
Preparation Time: 20 minutes

- ½ pound thin egg noodles *or* linguine
  Oriental Dressing
- 1 cup fresh bean sprouts
- 2 cups shredded lettuce
- 3 tablespoons sesame seed

Cook noodles in boiling salted water in wok until al dente or just tender; drain; toss with Dressing to prevent sticking. Just before serving, toss noodles with bean sprouts and lettuce. Sprinkle with sesame seed; serve immediately.

Oriental Dressing

- 2 tablespoons peanut butter
- 2 tablespoons water
- 2 tablespoons soy sauce
- 2 tablespoons vinegar
- 2 tablespoons peanut oil
- 1 tablespoon sesame oil
- 2 tablespoons minced green onion tops
- ½ teaspoon minced garlic
- ½ teaspoon peeled and minced fresh gingerroot
- 1 teaspoon salt

Combine all ingredients in jar; cover; shake to combine.

Flavored Rice, page 17;
Fried Rice with Ham, this page

Rice and Noodles

Sticky Rice

Makes 3 cups
Preparation Time: 20 minutes

        2 cups cold water
        1 teaspoon salt
        1 cup short-grain rice

Bring water to boil in wok; add salt and rice; stir. Reduce heat to medium; cover; cook 15 minutes or until water has evaporated.

Note: Cooked rice can be frozen and reheated in a microwave oven. Allow 1 minute on high power per 1 cup thawed rice.

Noodles in Oyster Sauce

Makes 4 servings
Preparation Time: 10 minutes

        ½ pound Chinese egg noodles
        ¼ cup peanut oil
        4 ¼-inch slices fresh gingerroot, peeled and grated
        4 green onions including tops, diagonally sliced in 1-inch pieces
        ½ cup chicken stock
          Oyster sauce to taste

Cook noodles in boiling water about 3 minutes; drain. Heat oil in wok until hot. Add gingerroot and green onions; stir-fry 2 minutes. Add stock; stir-fry over high heat until stock is reduced to 3 to 4 tablespoons. Add noodles; stir-fry until heated through. Stir in oyster sauce. Serve immediately.

Spanish Rice

Makes 6 to 8 servings
Preparation Time: 40 minutes

        4 cups chicken stock
        1 cup tomato sauce
        1 teaspoon salt
        1 tablespoon whole pickling spice
        2 cups long-grain rice
        2 tablespoons oil
          Chopped fresh tomato
          Chopped fresh green pepper

Mix first 3 ingredients in wok. Place pickling spice in cheesecloth bag; add to wok. Bring to boil; reduce heat; simmer 10 minutes. Sauté rice in hot oil in skillet or another wok until lightly browned. Add to stock mixture. Bring to boil; cover; simmer about 25 minutes or until rice is tender. Remove spice bag. Serve immediately garnished with chopped tomato and pepper.

Exotic Noodles

Makes 4 servings
Preparation Time: 15 minutes

        ¼ cup unsalted butter
        ½ pound Chinese egg noodles, cooked and drained
        ¼ cup toasted sesame seed
        ¼ cup soy sauce
        2 green onions, thinly sliced

Melt butter in wok over medium heat. (Do not use high heat or butter will burn.) Add next 3 ingredients; toss to combine; heat through. Sprinkle with green onions. Serve immediately.

Shrimp Fried Rice

Makes 4 servings
Preparation Time: 15 minutes; 7 minutes to cook

        2 tablespoons peanut oil
        ½ pound small shrimp, shelled
        ½ teaspoon sugar
        ½ teaspoon salt
        ½ cup thinly sliced green onions including tops
        ½ cup diced bamboo shoots
        2 cups cold cooked rice
        1 cup fresh bean sprouts
        3 tablespoons soy sauce
        3 eggs, lightly beaten

Heat oil in wok until hot. Add next 3 ingredients; stir-fry 2 to 3 minutes. Add green onions and bamboo shoots; stir-fry 1 minute. Add rice and bean sprouts; stir-fry 30 seconds. Add soy sauce; stir to mix. Make well in center of rice; pour in eggs; allow to set; scramble with spatula; stir into rice. Serve immediately.

Sesame Rice

Makes 4 servings
Preparation Time: 20 minutes

        1 tablespoon unsalted butter
        1 tablespoon peanut oil
        1 cup raw long-grain rice
        ¼ cup sesame seed
        2 cups chicken stock
        1 teaspoon salt
        ¼ teaspoon peeled and minced fresh gingerroot
        1 tablespoon soy sauce *or* more to taste

Melt butter in oil in wok over medium heat. Add rice and sesame seed; cook, stirring constantly, over low heat until light brown. Add stock, salt and gingerroot. Stir; bring to boil; cover; reduce heat to low; simmer 15 minutes. Uncover; stir in soy sauce. Serve immediately.

TEMPURA

Tempura is a Japanese frying technique in which small pieces or slices of food are dipped in a thin batter and fried in hot oil in a wok. The result is tender-crisp vegetables, seafood and meat encased in a delicate crunchy coating. The food can be cooked by one or two people in the kitchen just before serving, or the cooking can be done in an electric wok at the table. A variety of garnishes and dipping sauces are served.

To Prepare Tempura:

1. Have all foods for tempura frying cut in bite-size or thin strips, arranged attractively on a platter. Be sure foods are at room temperature before cooking.

2. Prepare the dipping sauces and seasonings to be served. These can be prepared hours in advance. They should be at room temperature when served.

3. Prepare either Batter I (it must stand at room temperature 1 hour) or Batter II (it must be prepared just before using and kept cold) or prepare both batters, if desired.

4. Heat 1 quart peanut oil in electric wok to 400° or so that oil reaches 365°. (If an electric wok is not available, use a wok on the stove and heat the oil to the prescribed temperature.) Fit the wok with a tempura ring if available. If not, line a plate with paper towels for draining excess oil from foods.

5. Using tongs or chopsticks, coat foods to be fried, one by one, with batter; drop into hot oil. Fry 3 or 4 items at a time, browning on all sides, 2 to 3 minutes. It will be necessary to increase the temperature of the oil during frying because its temperature will be lowered as foods are added. Remove cooked food with slotted spoon or strainer; place on tempura ring or paper towels to drain; serve while hot.

6. Each person dips the tempura-fried foods in the desired sauces. Food can be cooked by one person or everyone at the table. Divide batter so that each person has his own dish. If using the batter containing ice water, place individual bowls of this batter in bowls of crushed ice to keep it cold.

Suggested Ingredients:

Sweet potato, peeled, cut into ¼-inch-wide slices
Spanish onion, peeled, cut in ¼-inch-wide slices without separating into rings
Green or red pepper, cut in ½-inch-wide strips
Zucchini, unpeeled, cut in ⅛-inch-wide strips
Green beans, ends trimmed
Cucumber, peeled, thinly sliced
Parsley sprigs
Mushrooms, halved if particularly large
Eggplant, unpeeled, cut in thin strips
Celery, cut in 3-inch-long strips
Carrot, cut in 3-inch-long strips
Snow peas, ends and strings removed
Flounder or sole, cut in 2-inch pieces
Sea scallops, halved if particularly large
Shrimp, shelled except for tails, deveined
Chunks of lobster, 1½ inches
Chunks of boneless, skinned chicken breast, ½ inch
Chicken livers, halved

Dipping Sauces and Seasonings:

Soy sauce
Grated white radish
Lemon juice
Sweet and Sour Sauce (recipe on page 31)
Hot Mustard Sauce (recipe on page 31)
Plum Sauce (recipe on page 31)
Tempura Sauce (recipe on page 31)

Tempura

Batter I

> 2 eggs
> 1⅓ cups flour
> 1 teaspoon salt
> 1 cup flat beer

Beat eggs in bowl; add ⅓ cup flour and salt. Add beer alternately with remaining flour, beating after each addition. Let batter stand at room temperature 1 hour.

Batter II

> ⅔ cup flour
> 3 tablespoons cornstarch
> ½ teaspoon salt
> 2 eggs
> ¾ cup ice water

Stir first 3 ingredients together in bowl. Beat eggs and ice water in another bowl until blended. Add to flour mixture; stir until just moistened. Batter will be lumpy. Do not stir again. Keep batter cold by placing it in a bowl set in a larger bowl of crushed ice.

CHINESE HOT POT

A Chinese hot pot dinner is a fun way to entertain. To be authentic, a Mongolian hot pot should be used, but an electric wok will serve the purpose perfectly well. Chicken stock is heated to boiling in a wok. Guests then dip meat, seafood and vegetables into the stock using chopsticks or spearing food on bamboo skewers. These foods are then eaten with an assortment of sauces.

Then cellophane noodles are cooked in the stock, and the noodles and stock are ladled into serving bowls as the last course of the dinner. All of the preparation is done in advance, making this an almost effortless party menu. It's best to serve this to no more than four people at a time so each will have easy access to the wok.

Suggested Vegetables:

Broccoli flowerets, sliced ¼ inch thick
Cauliflowerets, sliced ¼ inch thick
Carrots, pared, cut in ⅛-inch-thick diagonal slices
Snow peas, ends and strings removed
Spinach leaves, washed, stems removed
Mushrooms, wiped clean, sliced ¼ inch thick

Green onions, roots removed, cut in 1½-inch-long pieces
Red or green pepper strips, ¼ inch wide

Suggested Proteins:

Pork tenderloin, beef top sirloin, lean lamb; all cut across grain in ⅛-inch-thick slices
Chicken breast, skinned and boned, cut across grain in ¼-inch-thick slices
Chicken livers, halved
Medium to large shrimp, shelled and deveined, halved lengthwise
Sea scallops, halved if particularly large
Tofu or bean curd, cut in ½- to 1-inch cubes

Other Ingredients:

3 to 4 ounces cellophane noodles
3 to 4 cups warm water
6 to 8 cups richly flavored chicken stock
Soy sauce
Teriyaki Sauce (recipe page 31)
Plum Sauce (recipe page 31)
Hoisin Sauce (recipe page 31)
Mustard Sauce (recipe page 31)

To Prepare Hot Pot:

Arrange vegetables and proteins attractively in overlapping layers on serving trays. Cover; refrigerate until serving time. Cover cellophane noodles with warm water; let stand 30 minutes. Drain; cut in 6-inch lengths. When ready to serve, put enough stock in wok to fill halfway. Heat to boiling. Let guests cook vegetables and proteins to desired doneness, 1 to 4 minutes. Serve with dipping sauces. It may be necessary to add additional stock to wok. As the last course, heat noodles in stock; ladle into bowls.

Vegetables

Harvest Vegetable Stir-Fry

Makes 6 to 8 servings
Preparation Time: 15 minutes; 15 minutes to cook

- 2 tablespoons peanut oil
- 1 ¼-inch slice fresh gingerroot, peeled
- 2 cups small broccoli flowerets, blanched 3 minutes
- 2 cups small cauliflowerets, blanched 3 minutes
- 2 cups sliced fresh mushrooms
- 1 green pepper, cored, seeded and cut in ¼-inch-wide strips
- 2 cups thin diagonal celery slices
- 1 large clove garlic, peeled and minced
- 1 teaspoon salt
- 1 teaspoon freshly ground black pepper
- 2 tablespoons soy sauce
- ½ cup grated sharp Cheddar cheese

Heat oil in wok until hot. Add gingerroot; swirl around sides of wok; discard. Add broccoli, cauliflower, mushrooms, green pepper and celery in that order. Add garlic, salt and pepper. Cover; cook 10 minutes or until vegetables are tender-crisp. Add soy sauce; toss. Sprinkle with cheese; cook until cheese melts. Serve immediately.

Julienne Vegetable Stir-Fry

Makes 6 servings
Preparation Time: 10 minutes; 4 minutes to cook

- 2 tablespoons peanut oil
- 1 small green pepper, cut in 1½-inch-long julienne strips
- 2 small carrots, pared, cut in 1½-inch-long julienne strips
- ½ rib celery, cut in 1½-inch-long julienne strips
- 1 unpeeled zucchini, cut in 1½-inch-long julienne strips
- 2 tablespoons chicken stock
- 20 snow peas, ends trimmed, strings removed
  Salt and freshly ground black pepper to taste

Heat oil in wok until hot. Add green pepper and carrots; stir-fry 1 minute. Add celery and zucchini; stir-fry 1 minute. Add stock; cover; cook 30 seconds. Add snow peas; cook 1 minute. Season with salt and black pepper. Serve immediately.

Stir-Fried Asparagus

Makes 4 servings
Preparation Time: 10 minutes; 6 minutes to cook

- 2 tablespoons peanut oil
- 2 cloves garlic, peeled and minced
- 1 cup chicken stock
- 1 pound asparagus, cut in 2-inch diagonal pieces, leaving tips whole
- 2 tablespoons dry sherry
- 2 tablespoons soy sauce
- 2 teaspoons cornstarch
- ¼ teaspoon sugar
- ¾ teaspoon salt
- ¼ teaspoon black pepper

Heat oil in wok until hot. Add garlic; stir-fry 10 seconds. Add stock and asparagus; bring to boil. Cover; cook 5 minutes or until asparagus is tender-crisp. Meanwhile, mix remaining ingredients. Uncover; stir cornstarch mixture; add to wok; stir-fry until sauce thickens. Serve immediately.

Stir-Fried Broccoli

Makes 4 servings
Preparation Time: 10 minutes; 3 minutes to cook

- 2½ tablespoons peanut oil
- 1 clove garlic, peeled and split lengthwise
- 1 pound broccoli, cut in 1½-inch pieces
- ½ teaspoon salt
- ¼ teaspoon freshly ground black pepper
- 2 1-inch-long dried chilies, crushed
- 2 tablespoons cold water
- ½ teaspoon sesame oil

Heat oil in wok until hot. Add garlic; swirl around wok 30 seconds; discard. Add next 4 ingredients; stir-fry 1 minute. Add water; cover; cook 1 minute. Uncover; add sesame oil; stir-fry 30 seconds. Serve immediately.

Stir-Fried Spinach

Makes 3 to 4 servings
Preparation Time: 10 minutes; 3 minutes to cook

- 2 tablespoons peanut oil
- 1 clove garlic, peeled
- 1 pound fresh spinach, washed, stems discarded
- ½ teaspoon salt
  Pinch sugar

Heat oil in wok until hot. Add garlic and spinach; stir-fry 1 minute. Discard garlic. Add salt and sugar; stir-fry 1 minute. Serve immediately.

Sweet and Sour Zucchini

Makes 4 servings
Preparation Time: 10 minutes; 10 minutes to cook

    2 tablespoons peanut oil
    3 unpeeled medium zucchini, cut in ½-inch slices
    2 tablespoons sugar dissolved in
      2 tablespoons vinegar
      Salt and freshly ground white pepper to taste

Heat oil in wok until hot. Add zucchini; stir-fry until tender-crisp. Add remaining ingredients; simmer 3 minutes. Serve immediately.

Stir-Fried Green Beans

Makes 4 servings
Preparation Time: 10 minutes; 4 minutes to cook

    2 tablespoons peanut oil
    2 small cloves garlic, peeled and finely chopped
    2 ¼-inch slices fresh gingerroot, peeled and
      finely chopped
    2 green onions, thinly sliced
    1 pound green beans, ends removed,
      blanched 4 minutes
      Salt to taste

Heat oil in wok until hot. Add next 3 ingredients; stir-fry 30 seconds. Add beans; stir-fry 2 to 3 minutes or until tender-crisp. Add salt. Serve immediately.

Stir-Fried Vegetables on Rice Sticks

Makes 4 servings
Preparation Time: 20 minutes; 7 minutes to cook

    ¼ cup peanut oil
    3 to 4 ounces rice sticks, torn into 2 batches
    2 ribs celery, cut in thin diagonal slices
   20 snow peas, ends and strings removed
   10 Chinese dried black mushrooms, soaked in hot
      water 20 minutes, drained, stems discarded, caps
      thinly sliced
    2 cups fresh bean sprouts
    1 tablespoon curry powder mixed with
      1 cup chicken stock
      Salt to taste

Heat oil in wok until hot. Add 1 batch rice sticks; cook until puffed; turn; cook 10 seconds on other side. Remove to paper towel to drain. Cook remaining batch rice sticks in same manner. Remove all but 1 tablespoon oil from wok. Heat oil in wok until hot. Add celery, snow peas, mushrooms and bean sprouts; stir-fry 2 minutes. Add curry powder mixture and salt. Pour over rice sticks. Serve immediately.

Vegetable Stir-Fry

Makes 4 servings
Preparation Time: 10 minutes; 6 minutes to cook

    2 tablespoons peanut oil
    1 clove garlic, peeled and minced
    1 ¼-inch slice fresh gingerroot, peeled and minced
    1 small onion, peeled and cut into thin rings
    1 cup small cauliflowerets, blanched in boiling water
      until almost tender
    1 cup small broccoli flowerets, blanched in boiling
      water until almost tender
    4 to 5 fresh mushrooms, wiped clean, halved
      Salt to taste

Heat oil in wok until hot. Add garlic, gingerroot and onion; stir-fry until onion is limp, about 2 minutes. Add cauliflower, broccoli and mushrooms; stir-fry 3 to 4 minutes or until vegetables are tender-crisp. Add salt; serve immediately.

Vegetable Stir-Fry Deluxe

Makes 6 servings
Preparation Time: 20 minutes; 7 minutes to cook

    2 tablespoons peanut oil
    2 onions, peeled, halved vertically and sliced
    2 green peppers, cored, seeded and cut in thin strips
    2 carrots, pared and cut in thin diagonal slices
    2 ribs celery, cut in thin diagonal slices
    1 ¼-inch slice fresh gingerroot, peeled and minced
    3 cloves garlic, peeled and finely chopped
    2 tablespoons soy sauce
    2 tablespoons dry sherry
    1 pound broccoli flowerets, blanched 3 minutes
    ½ pound cauliflowerets, blanched 3 minutes
    1 cup shredded bok choy (Chinese cabbage)
    1 cup fresh bean sprouts
    2 tablespoons fresh lemon juice
      Salt and freshly ground black pepper to taste

Heat oil in wok until hot. Add next 3 ingredients; stir-fry 3 minutes. Add next 5 ingredients; stir-fry 2 minutes. Add broccoli and cauliflower; stir-fry 1 minute. Add cabbage; stir-fry 30 seconds. Add bean sprouts and lemon juice; stir-fry to heat through. Season with salt and pepper. Serve immediately.

Snow Peas with Water Chestnuts

Makes 4 servings
Preparation Time: 10 minutes; 2 minutes to cook

- 2 tablespoons peanut oil
- 1 ¼-inch slice fresh gingerroot, peeled
- 1 pound snow peas, ends and strings removed
- 1 teaspoon salt
- 1 tablespoon water
- 1 8-ounce can sliced water chestnuts, drained
- ½ teaspoon sugar

Heat oil in wok until hot. Add gingerroot; swirl around wok 30 seconds; discard. Add snow peas; stir-fry 30 seconds. Add salt and water; cover; cook 30 seconds. Uncover; add water chestnuts and sugar; stir-fry 30 seconds. Serve immediately.

Vegetables and Cashew Nuts

Makes 4 servings
Preparation Time: 15 minutes; 4 minutes to cook

- 2 tablespoons peanut oil
- 1 cup diagonally sliced celery
- 1 small red onion, peeled and sliced
- 1 cup sliced water chestnuts, drained
- 20 snow peas, ends and strings removed
- 1 clove garlic, peeled and crushed
- 1 teaspoon sugar
- 1 tablespoon soy sauce
- ½ cup chicken stock
- 1 cup unsalted cashew nuts
- 1 teaspoon cornstarch mixed with
  - 1 tablespoon cold water

Heat oil in wok until hot. Stir-fry celery and onion 15 seconds. Add next 6 ingredients; stir-fry 1 minute. Add nuts. Stir cornstarch mixture; add to wok. Stir-fry until thickened. Serve immediately.

Stir-Fried Zucchini

Makes 4 servings
Preparation Time: 5 minutes; 10 minutes to cook

- 2 tablespoons peanut oil
- 2 medium onions, peeled and thinly sliced
- 4 unpeeled medium zucchini, cut in
  - ½-inch diagonal slices
  - Salt and freshly ground black pepper to taste
- ½ teaspoon dried basil
- ½ teaspoon dried oregano
- 1 clove garlic, peeled and crushed
- 1 tablespoon chopped fresh parsley

Heat oil in wok until hot. Add onion; stir-fry until limp. Add zucchini; cook 4 minutes. Add remaining ingredients; lower heat; cook 4 minutes. Serve immediately.

Ginger Stir-Fried Vegetables, this page;
Vegetable Stir-Fry Deluxe, page 25

Ginger Stir-Fried Vegetables

Makes 4 servings
Preparation Time: 10 minutes; 5 minutes to cook

- 2 tablespoons peanut oil
- 1 teaspoon peeled and minced fresh gingerroot
- 1 clove garlic, peeled and minced
- ¼ pound cauliflowerets, cut in ¼-inch slices
- 1 cup pared and thinly sliced carrots
- ⅓ cup chicken stock
- ¼ pound asparagus, cut in 1½-inch pieces
- ¼ pound snow peas, ends and strings removed
- ½ teaspoon salt
- ½ teaspoon sesame oil

Heat oil in wok until hot. Add gingerroot and garlic; stir-fry 30 seconds. Add cauliflower, carrots and chicken stock; cover; cook 2 minutes. Uncover; add asparagus; cover; cook 1 minute. Uncover; add snow peas; stir-fry 30 seconds. Add salt and sesame oil; stir-fry 30 seconds. Serve immediately.

Mushroom and Broccoli Stir-Fry

Makes 8 servings
Preparation Time: 15 minutes; 20 minutes to cook

- 3 tablespoons peanut oil
- ½ cup chopped onion
- 1 pound fresh mushrooms, wiped clean, halved
- 1 pound small broccoli flowerets
- 1 clove garlic, peeled and minced
- ⅓ cup sliced water chestnuts, drained
- 1 tablespoon cornstarch
- ½ teaspoon salt
- 1 ¼-inch slice fresh gingerroot, peeled and minced
- 1 tablespoon soy sauce
- ¾ cup chicken stock

Heat 1 tablespoon oil in wok until hot. Add onion; stir-fry 2 minutes. Add mushrooms; stir-fry 3 minutes. Remove from wok; set aside. Heat 2 tablespoons oil in wok until hot. Add broccoli and garlic; stir-fry 3 minutes. Add water chestnuts; stir-fry 2 minutes. Blend remaining ingredients; pour in wok. Cook until mixture thickens. Reduce heat; simmer, covered, until broccoli is tender-crisp, about 5 minutes. Return sautéed mushrooms to wok. Heat through. Serve immediately.

Vegetables

Green Beans with Water Chestnuts

Makes 4 servings
Preparation Time: 15 minutes; 8 minutes to cook

- 1 teaspoon peanut oil
- 1 teaspoon sesame oil
- ½ pound green beans, cut diagonally in 1½-inch pieces
- ½ cup sliced water chestnuts, drained
- ½ cup sliced fresh mushrooms
- 1 small clove garlic, peeled and crushed
- 2 tablespoons soy sauce
- 2 tablespoons cold water
- ½ teaspoon salt
- ¼ teaspoon freshly ground black pepper
- 2 teaspoons sesame seed

Heat both oils in wok until hot. Add next 4 ingredients; stir-fry 1 minute. Add remaining ingredients; cover; cook until beans are tender, 5 to 7 minutes. Serve immediately.

Stir-Fried Broccoli and Carrots

Makes 6 servings
Preparation Time: 15 minutes; 5 minutes to cook

- 2 tablespoons peanut oil
- 2 ¼-inch slices gingerroot, peeled and finely chopped
- 1 clove garlic, peeled and finely chopped
- 1½ cups small broccoli flowerets
- 1½ cups pared and thinly sliced carrots
- 1 small onion, peeled, sliced and separated into rings
- ¾ cup chicken stock
- 1 teaspoon salt
- 1 tablespoon cornstarch mixed with 2 tablespoons cold water
- 1 8-ounce can sliced water chestnuts, drained
- 1 cup sliced fresh mushrooms
- 2 tablespoons oyster sauce

Heat oil in wok until hot. Add gingerroot and garlic; stir-fry 15 seconds. Add next 3 ingredients; stir-fry 1 minute. Add chicken stock and salt; cover; cook until carrots are tender-crisp, about 3 minutes. Stir cornstarch mixture; add to vegetable mixture. Cook, stirring, until slightly thickened, about 10 seconds. Add remaining ingredients; stir-fry 30 seconds. Serve immediately.

Green Bean and Zucchini Stir-Fry

Makes 4 servings
Preparation Time: 10 minutes; 10 minutes to cook

- 2 tablespoons peanut oil
- 1 pound fresh green beans, cut in 2-inch pieces
- 3 cups unpeeled sliced zucchini
- ¼ cup chopped celery
- 1 tablespoon fresh lemon juice
- 1½ teaspoons salt
- ⅓ cup chicken stock
- 1 teaspoon cornstarch dissolved in 1 tablespoon water

Heat oil in wok until hot. Add beans; stir-fry 3 minutes or until tender-crisp. Add next 4 ingredients; stir-fry 3 minutes. Add stock; cover; simmer 3 minutes. Stir cornstarch mixture; add to wok. Serve immediately.

Broccoli and Cauliflower with Garlic

Makes 4 servings
Preparation Time: 10 minutes; 5 minutes to cook

- 2 tablespoons peanut oil
- 2 small cloves garlic, peeled and crushed
- 2 cups small broccoli flowerets, blanched 3 minutes
- 2 cups small cauliflowerets, blanched 3 minutes
- 1 cup chicken stock
- 2 teaspoons cornstarch mixed with 2 teaspoons cold water

Heat oil in wok until hot. Add garlic; stir-fry 30 seconds. Add broccoli and cauliflower; stir-fry 2 minutes. Add stock; cover; cook 2 minutes or until vegetables are tender-crisp. Stir cornstarch mixture; add to wok; stir-fry until sauce thickens slightly. Serve immediately.

Broccoli Cantonese

Makes 4 servings
Preparation Time: 10 minutes; 5 to 7 minutes to cook

- 2 tablespoons peanut oil
- 1½ pounds small broccoli flowerets
- 1 cup chicken stock
- 2 teaspoons cornstarch
- 2 teaspoons cold water
- 1 ¼-inch slice fresh gingerroot, peeled and minced
- ½ teaspoon salt
- ¼ teaspoon sesame oil

Heat oil in wok until hot. Add broccoli and stock; bring to boil. Cover; cook 3 to 5 minutes or until broccoli is tender-crisp. Meanwhile, mix next 4 ingredients. Uncover wok; stir cornstarch mixture; add to wok. Stir-fry until sauce thickens. Add sesame oil; stir-fry 10 seconds. Serve immediately.

Stir-Fried Peppers

Makes 4 servings
Preparation Time: 15 minutes; 7 minutes to cook

2 tablespoons olive oil
2 green peppers, cored, seeded, cut in ½-inch-wide
  lengthwise strips
2 red peppers, cored, seeded, cut in ½-inch-wide
  lengthwise strips
1 large clove garlic, peeled and crushed
1 medium onion, peeled, thinly sliced and separated
  into rings
½ teaspoon crumbled oregano
  Pinch cayenne pepper
3 to 4 dashes hot pepper sauce
  Salt and freshly ground black pepper to taste

Heat oil in wok until hot. Add pepper strips; stir-fry 2 minutes. Add remaining ingredients; stir-fry 30 seconds. Cover; simmer 3 to 4 minutes or until peppers are tender-crisp. Serve immediately.

Note: If red peppers are not available, substitute green peppers.

Garden Stir-Fry

Makes 4 servings
Preparation Time: 20 minutes; 8 minutes to cook

2 tablespoons peanut oil
½ pound fresh mushrooms, wiped clean, thinly sliced
  Salt and freshly ground black pepper to taste
1 tablespoon fresh lemon juice
2 small onions, peeled, halved vertically and sliced
1 large green pepper, cored, seeded and
  cut in thin strips
2 large cloves garlic, peeled and crushed
1 teaspoon dried rosemary, crumbled
1 teaspoon dried basil
½ teaspoon dried marjoram
  Salt and freshly ground black pepper to taste
2 tablespoons dry red wine
2 medium unpeeled zucchini, cut in
  thin diagonal slices
2 small tomatoes, cored, each cut in 6 wedges

Heat 1 tablespoon oil in wok until hot. Add mushrooms; sprinkle with salt and pepper to taste and lemon juice. Stir-fry 2 minutes; remove; set aside. Heat remaining 1 tablespoon oil in wok until hot. Add next 3 ingredients; stir-fry 2 minutes. Add seasonings, wine, zucchini, tomatoes and mushrooms; stir-fry 2 minutes. Serve immediately.

Bean Sprout and Mushroom Stir-Fry

Makes 4 servings
Preparation Time: 20 minutes; 6 minutes to cook

2 tablespoons peanut oil
6 to 8 Chinese dried black mushrooms, soaked in hot
  water 20 minutes, drained, stems discarded, caps
  thinly sliced
3½ cups fresh bean sprouts
1 clove garlic, peeled and finely chopped
1 teaspoon peeled and finely chopped fresh
  gingerroot
½ cup water
2 teaspoons cornstarch mixed with
  1 tablespoon cold water
1 tablespoon soy sauce
2 green onions, cut in 1-inch pieces

Heat oil in wok until hot. Add mushrooms, bean sprouts, garlic and gingerroot; stir-fry 2 minutes. Add water; bring to boil. Stir cornstarch mixture; add to wok with soy sauce. Stir until thickened. Garnish with green onions. Serve immediately.

Cauliflower Stir-Fry

Makes 4 servings
Preparation Time: 5 minutes; 15 minutes to cook

3 tablespoons peanut oil
1 small head cauliflower, separated into
  small flowerets
2 tablespoons fresh lemon juice
2 tablespoons water
4 green onions, thinly sliced
1 clove garlic, peeled and crushed
  Salt and freshly ground white pepper to taste

Heat 1 tablespoon oil in wok until hot. Add next 3 ingredients; cover; cook on medium heat 7 to 10 minutes or until crisp-tender. Remove from wok with strainer; set aside. Heat remaining 2 tablespoons oil in wok until hot. Add green onions; stir-fry 30 seconds. Add garlic; stir-fry 30 seconds. Add cauliflower, salt and pepper. Stir-fry 1 minute. Cook 2 minutes. Serve immediately.

Hot Mustard Sauce I

Makes 1 cup
Preparation Time: 15 minutes

¼ cup dry mustard
2 tablespoons peanut oil
2 tablespoons water
¼ cup sugar
1 tablespoon cornstarch
½ teaspoon salt
½ cup water
¼ cup white vinegar

Mix mustard and oil in small bowl. Gradually add 2 tablespoons water, stirring constantly, to form smooth paste. Stir together sugar, cornstarch and salt in wok; gradually add ½ cup water and vinegar. Blend thoroughly. Cook over medium heat, stirring constantly, until mixture thickens. Gradually add to mustard mixture, stirring constantly, until blended. Refrigerate until serving time. Stir before serving. Serve at room temperature.

Hot Mustard Sauce II

Makes approximately ⅓ cup
Preparation Time: 2 minutes; 30 minutes for flavors to blend

3 tablespoons dry mustard
2 tablespoons water
1 tablespoon soy sauce

Stir all ingredients together until smooth; let set 30 minutes for flavors to blend before serving.

Plum Sauce

Makes approximately 1 cup
Preparation Time: 15 minutes

1 cup plum jam, jelly *or* preserves
½ cup applesauce
½ teaspoon ground ginger
2 teaspoons cornstarch
2 teaspoons soy sauce
2 teaspoons wine vinegar

Mix plum jam and applesauce in wok; bring to boil over medium heat. Combine ginger, cornstarch, soy sauce, vinegar; stir into jam mixture. Cook, stirring constantly, until mixture thickens. Cool. Refrigerate until serving time. Bring to room temperature before serving.

Ginger Sauce

Makes approximately ¾ cup
Preparation Time: 2 minutes

1 tablespoon ground ginger
1 small clove garlic, peeled and crushed
¼ cup water
2 tablespoons sugar
½ cup soy sauce

Mix all ingredients. Use as dipping sauce.

Sweet and Sour Sauce

Makes approximately 1¼ cups
Preparation Time: 5 minutes

½ cup pineapple juice
½ cup white wine vinegar
2 tablespoons peanut oil
2 tablespoons packed light brown sugar
1 tablespoon soy sauce
½ teaspoon freshly ground black pepper
2 teaspoons cornstarch mixed with
4 teaspoons cold water

Mix first 6 ingredients in wok; bring to boil. Stir cornstarch mixture; add to wok, stirring until sauce is clear and slightly thickened.

Tempura Sauce

Makes approximately ½ cup
Preparation Time: 10 minutes

¼ cup chicken stock
1 tablespoon soy sauce
1 tablespoon cream sherry
1 tablespoon grated daikon (Japanese radish)
1 tablespoon peeled and grated fresh gingerroot

Combine first 3 ingredients. Just before serving, stir in daikon and gingerroot.

Teriyaki Sauce

Makes approximately ⅔ cup
Preparation Time: 10 minutes

½ cup pineapple juice
¼ cup packed light brown sugar
2 tablespoons soy sauce
1 tablespoon peanut oil
¾ teaspoon ground ginger
¼ teaspoon salt
1 clove garlic, peeled and minced

Mix all ingredients in wok; heat to blend flavors.

Clockwise, from top:
Plum Sauce, this page;
Sweet and Sour Sauce, this page;
Hot Mustard Sauce, this page

Beef

Asparagus and Beef Stir-Fry

Makes 2 servings
Preparation Time: 15 minutes; 6 minutes to cook

- 1 tablespoon cornstarch
- ½ teaspoon sugar
- 1 tablespoon cold water
- 1 tablespoon hot bean sauce
- 1 clove garlic, peeled and crushed
- 3 tablespoons peanut oil
- ½ pound flank steak, thinly sliced across grain and cut in 1½-inch-long strips
- 1 pound asparagus, cut in ½-inch diagonal slices, blanched 2 minutes and drained
- 1½ teaspoons salt

Mix first 3 ingredients; set aside. Mix bean sauce and garlic; set aside. Heat 2 tablespoons oil in wok until hot. Add beef; stir-fry 1 minute; remove with strainer. Add remaining 1 tablespoon oil to wok; heat until hot. Add bean mixture; stir-fry 10 seconds. Add asparagus and salt; stir-fry 1 minute. Return meat to wok; stir cornstarch mixture; add to wok; stir-fry until slightly thickened. Serve immediately.

Beef Kwangton

Makes 4 servings
Preparation Time: 15 minutes; 4 minutes to cook

- 2 tablespoons peanut oil
- 1 ½-inch piece fresh gingerroot, peeled
- 1 pound lean flank or sirloin steak, thinly sliced across grain and cut in 1½-inch-long strips
- ½ cup sliced bamboo shoots, drained
- 4 large fresh mushrooms, wiped clean, thinly sliced
- 20 snow peas, ends and strings removed
- ½ cup chicken stock
- 2 tablespoons oyster sauce
- ½ teaspoon soy sauce
- ¼ teaspoon sesame oil
- ¼ teaspoon sugar
- ½ teaspoon salt
- 1 tablespoon cornstarch mixed with 1 tablespoon cold water

Heat oil in wok until hot. Swirl gingerroot in oil around wok 30 seconds; discard gingerroot. Add beef; stir-fry 2 minutes. Add next 4 ingredients; cover; cook 2 minutes. Meanwhile, mix next 5 ingredients. Uncover; add oyster sauce mixture and cornstarch mixture; stir-fry until sauce thickens. Serve immediately.

Cauliflower and Beef Chinoise

Makes 4 to 6 servings
Preparation Time: 20 minutes; 6 minutes to cook

- 3 tablespoons peanut oil
- 1 pound lean flank or sirloin steak, thinly sliced across grain and cut in 1½-inch-long strips
- 1 small onion, peeled, halved and thinly sliced
- 2 cloves garlic, peeled and minced
- 1 cup beef stock
- 1 small head cauliflower, cut into uniform-size flowerets
- 1 cup frozen peas
- ½ cup fresh bean sprouts
- ½ cup sliced bamboo shoots, drained
- 1 teaspoon salt
- 2 tablespoons cornstarch
- 1 tablespoon soy sauce
- ½ cup water
- 2 teaspoons dry sherry

Heat oil in wok until hot. Add beef, onion and garlic; stir-fry until meat begins to brown. Add next 6 ingredients; cover; cook until vegetables are barely tender, about 6 minutes. Mix remaining ingredients. Stir; add to wok; stir-fry until sauce thickens slightly. Serve immediately.

Chinese Pepper Steak

Makes 4 servings
Preparation Time: 15 minutes; 5 minutes to cook

- 1 tablespoon cornstarch
- 1 cup beef stock
- 1 tablespoon soy sauce
- 2 tablespoons peanut oil
- 1 pound round steak, thinly sliced and cut in 1½-inch-long strips
- 1 clove garlic, peeled and minced
- 2 small onions, peeled and each cut into 6 wedges
- 2 green peppers, cored, seeded and cut into thin 1½-inch-long strips
- 1 teaspoon salt
- ¼ teaspoon freshly ground black pepper
- ½ teaspoon peeled and minced fresh gingerroot

Mix first 3 ingredients; set aside. Heat oil in wok until hot. Add meat and garlic; stir-fry 1 minute. Add onion and peppers; stir-fry 1 to 2 minutes. Add next 3 ingredients. Stir cornstarch mixture; add to wok; stir-fry until sauce thickens slightly. Serve immediately.

Stir-Fried Beef and Snow Peas in Oyster Sauce

Makes 4 servings
Preparation Time: 30 minutes; 5 minutes to cook

    12 ¼-inch-thick slices beef tenderloin from large end,
       thinly sliced into strips
     2 tablespoons soy sauce
     2 tablespoons dry sherry
     ½ teaspoon ground Szechwan peppercorns
     ½ teaspoon peeled and grated fresh gingerroot
     ¼ cup oyster sauce
     2 tablespoons water
     2 tablespoons soy sauce
     2 tablespoons dry sherry
     1 teaspoon cornstarch
     1 teaspoon sesame oil
     2 tablespoons peanut oil
     1 ¼-inch slice fresh gingerroot, peeled
     ½ pound snow peas, ends and strings removed
     2 green onions, thinly sliced
     3 tablespoons water
     1 tablespoon dry sherry
     ½ teaspoon sugar
     ½ teaspoon salt
     1 teaspoon cornstarch mixed with
       1 teaspoon cold water

Mix first 5 ingredients in bowl; set aside to marinate 30 minutes. Mix next 6 ingredients; set aside. Heat oil in wok until hot. Add gingerroot slice; swirl around wok 30 seconds; discard. Add meat mixture and reserved oyster sauce mixture; stir-fry until meat loses pinkness, 2 to 3 minutes. Add next 6 ingredients; stir-fry 1 minute. Stir cornstarch mixture; add to wok; stir-fry until sauce thickens slightly. Serve immediately.

Stir-Fried Broccoli and Beef

Makes 4 servings
Preparation Time: 15 minutes; 8 minutes to cook

     2 teaspoons dry sherry
     ⅛ teaspoon freshly ground black pepper
     2 teaspoons soy sauce
     ½ teaspoon salt
     ½ teaspoon sugar
     ¾ cup water
     2 teaspoons cornstarch
     ¼ cup peanut oil
     ¾ pound broccoli, flowerets removed and reserved;
       stalks cut diagonally into ¼-inch slices
     ½ pound flank steak, thinly sliced across grain and cut
       in 1½-inch-long strips

Mix first 5 ingredients and ½ cup water; set aside. Mix cornstarch with remaining ¼ cup water; set aside. Heat 2 tablespoons oil in wok until hot. Add broccoli stalk slices; cover; cook 2 minutes. Add flowerets; cover; cook 2 minutes or until tender-crisp. Remove broccoli to hot platter. Add remaining 2 tablespoons oil to wok; heat until hot. Add meat; stir-fry 1 minute. Add soy sauce mixture; stir-fry 2 minutes. Return broccoli to wok; mix. Add cornstarch mixture; stir until slightly thickened. Serve immediately.

Sukiyaki

Makes 6 servings
Preparation Time: 20 minutes; 6 minutes to cook

     3 tablespoons peanut oil
     2 pounds top sirloin *or* boned and trimmed rib steak,
       cut in thin strips
       Sukiyaki Sauce
     3 bunches green onions, cut in 1½-inch-long strips
     2 pounds onions, peeled and sliced lengthwise into
       thin wedges
     2 bunches spinach, washed and stems discarded
     ¼ pound tofu, cut in small cubes
     ½ cup sliced bamboo shoots, drained
     ½ pound fresh bean sprouts
     ½ pound fresh mushrooms, sliced
     6 ribs celery, cut in thin diagonal slices

Heat oil in wok until hot. Add meat; stir-fry 1 minute. Add one-half of Sukiyaki Sauce and remaining ingredients. Stir-fry 3 to 4 minutes or until vegetables are tender-crisp. Add remaining sauce; stir-fry 1 minute. Serve immediately.

Sukiyaki Sauce

     ⅔ cup soy sauce
     ⅔ cup beef consommé
     1 tablespoon sugar
     ¼ cup sake *or* dry sherry

Stir all ingredients in bowl until sugar dissolves.

Tenderloin Stir-Fry

Makes 4 servings
Preparation Time: 15 minutes; 5 minutes to cook

     1 tablespoon cornstarch
     ½ cup cold water
     1 teaspoon soy sauce
     ½ teaspoon oyster sauce
     1 tablespoon peanut oil
     1 pound beef tenderloin, cut in 1-inch cubes
     8 large fresh mushrooms, wiped clean and sliced
     ½ teaspoon salt
     4 water chestnuts, sliced
     ¼ pound snow peas, ends and strings removed
     ¼ cup chicken stock

Mix first 4 ingredients; set aside. Heat oil in wok until hot. Add next 3 ingredients; stir-fry 2 minutes. Add remaining ingredients; stir-fry 1 minute. Stir cornstarch mixture; add to wok; stir-fry 1 to 2 minutes. Serve immediately.

Beef

Curried Beef and Vegetables

Makes 6 servings
Preparation Time: 20 minutes; 6 minutes to cook

- ¼ teaspoon peeled and minced fresh gingerroot
- ½ teaspoon sugar
- 1 tablespoon soy sauce
- 1 tablespoon curry powder
- ½ cup beef stock
- 2 tablespoons peanut oil
- 1 pound tenderloin, cut in ¼-inch-thick slices, cut across the grain in thin strips
- 1 medium onion, peeled, quartered and separated into layers
- 1 medium tomato, cored and cut in 6 wedges
- 1 green pepper, halved, cored, seeds removed and cut in thin 1½-inch-long strips
- 2 teaspoons cornstarch mixed with
  1 tablespoon cold water

Mix first 5 ingredients; set aside. Heat oil in wok over high heat until hot. Add meat; stir-fry 30 seconds; remove; set aside. Add next 3 ingredients; stir-fry 1 minute. Add curry mixture; cover; cook 2 to 3 minutes. Return meat to wok; stir together. Stir cornstarch mixture; add to wok; stir-fry until slightly thickened. Serve immediately.

Curry Beef

Makes 4 servings
Preparation Time: 15 minutes; 3½ minutes to cook

- 2 tablespoons peanut oil
- ½ pound lean flank steak, thinly sliced across grain and cut in 1½-inch-long strips
- 1 medium onion, peeled, quartered and cut in thin strips
- 1 small green pepper, cored, seeded and cut in thin 1½-inch-long strips
- 2 medium tomatoes, cored and each cut into 6 wedges
- ¼ cup chicken stock
- 1 teaspoon curry powder
- 1½ teaspoons sugar
- ½ teaspoon salt
- 1 tablespoon cornstarch mixed with
  1 tablespoon cold water

Heat oil in wok until hot. Add beef; stir-fry 30 seconds. Add next 4 ingredients; cover; cook on medium heat 2 minutes. Uncover; add curry powder, sugar and salt; stir-fry 30 seconds. Stir cornstarch mixture; add to wok. Stir-fry until sauce thickens. Serve immediately.

Hot and Spicy Beef

Makes 4 to 6 servings
Preparation Time: 20 minutes; 4 minutes to cook

- 1 pound flank steak, thinly sliced across grain and cut in 1½-inch-long strips
- 1 egg, lightly beaten
- 1 teaspoon baking soda
- 3 tablespoons peanut oil
- 1 tablespoon cornstarch mixed with
  1 tablespoon cold water
- 2 tablespoons peanut oil
- 1 small red pepper, cored, seeded and cut into thin 1½-inch-long strips
- 1 small green pepper, cored, seeded and cut into thin 1½-inch-long strips
- ½ cup sliced water chestnuts, drained
- 1 tablespoon dry sherry
- 2 small dried chilies, crushed
- 1 tablespoon soy sauce
- ½ teaspoon sugar
- ½ teaspoon salt
- ¼ teaspoon sesame oil
- 1 tablespoon cornstarch mixed with
  1 tablespoon cold water

Mix meat with next 4 ingredients in small bowl; set aside to marinate at least 20 minutes. Heat oil in wok until hot. Add meat mixture; stir-fry 1 minute. Add next 3 ingredients; stir-fry 1 minute. Add next 6 ingredients; stir-fry 1 minute. Stir cornstarch mixture; add to wok. Stir-fry until sauce thickens. Serve immediately.

Mongolian Beef

Makes 4 servings
Preparation Time: 15 minutes; 3½ minutes to cook

- 1 pound lean flank *or* sirloin steak, thinly sliced across grain and cut in 1½-inch-long strips
- 2 tablespoons soy sauce
- ½ teaspoon salt
- 1 tablespoon dry sherry
- ½ teaspoon dried red pepper flakes
- 3 tablespoons peanut oil
- 1 tablespoon sesame oil
- ½ teaspoon chopped garlic
- 1 bunch green onions, each cut in half lengthwise, then cut diagonally in 1-inch-long pieces

Put meat strips in bowl; add 1 tablespoon soy sauce, next 3 ingredients and 2 tablespoons oil; set aside. Mix remaining 1 tablespoon soy sauce with sesame oil; set aside. Heat remaining 1 tablespoon oil in wok until hot. Add garlic; stir-fry 10 seconds. Add beef; stir-fry 1 minute. Add onion and sesame oil mixture; stir-fry until heated through, 1 to 2 minutes. Serve immediately.

Oriental Beef with Vegetables, page 37

Beef

Oriental Meatball Dinner

Makes 4 servings
Preparation Time: 30 minutes; 6 to 7 minutes to cook

- ½ pound very lean ground beef
- ½ pound mild pork sausage
- 1 cup beef stock
- ½ cup water chestnuts, drained and chopped
- 1 egg, lightly beaten
- ⅓ cup quick-cooking rolled oats
- 2 tablespoons chopped onion
- 1½ teaspoons toasted sesame seed
- 1 teaspoon salt
- ¾ teaspoon peeled and minced fresh gingerroot
- 2 tablespoons peanut oil
- 1 unpeeled small zucchini, thinly sliced
- 1 small green pepper, cored, seeded and cut into thin 1-inch-long strips
- 1 small onion, peeled, sliced and separated into rings
- 2 ribs celery, cut in thin diagonal slices
- 2 cloves garlic, peeled and minced
- 1 cup fresh bean sprouts
- ⅓ cup water
- 2 tablespoons soy sauce mixed with 1½ tablespoons cornstarch

Preheat oven to 450°. Mix beef, sausage, ½ cup stock and next 7 ingredients in bowl. Use 2 tablespoons mixture to shape into smooth ball; place on ungreased baking sheet. Repeat with remaining meat mixture, placing meatballs on sheet so they do not touch. Bake 30 minutes; remove; keep warm. Heat oil in wok until hot. Add next 5 ingredients; stir-fry 3 minutes. Add bean sprouts; stir-fry 1 minute. Add meatballs, remaining ½ cup stock and water; bring to simmer. Stir cornstarch mixture; add to wok; stir gently until sauce thickens slightly. Serve immediately.

Stir-Fried Beef and Bean Sauce

Makes 2 servings
Preparation Time: 15 minutes; 4 minutes to cook

- 1 small red or green pepper, cored, seeded and cut in 1-inch pieces
- 1 small onion, peeled and cut into rings
- 2 ¼-inch slices fresh gingerroot, peeled and minced
- 1 clove garlic, peeled and minced
- 1 tablespoon dry sherry
- 1 tablespoon water
- 1 tablespoon cornstarch
- ½ cup beef stock
- 2 tablespoons peanut oil
- ½ pound flank or sirloin steak, thinly sliced across grain and cut in 1½-inch-long strips
- 2 tablespoons bean sauce

Combine pepper and onion; set aside. Combine gingerroot and garlic; set aside. Mix next 4 ingredients; set aside. Heat oil in wok until hot. Add gingerroot and garlic; stir-fry 30 seconds. Add pepper and onion; stir-fry 2 minutes. Add beef; stir-fry 1 minute or until beef is browned. Add bean sauce; stir-fry 30 seconds. Stir cornstarch mixture; add to wok; stir-fry until slightly thickened. Serve immediately.

Stir-Fried Round Steak and Vegetables

Makes 4 servings
Preparation Time: 15 minutes; 4 minutes to cook

- 2 tablespoons peanut oil
- 1 pound round steak, thinly sliced across grain and cut in 1½-inch-long strips
- 3 tablespoons soy sauce
- 1 head bok choy, thinly sliced (Chinese cabbage)
- ¼ pound fresh mushrooms, sliced
- 1 8-ounce can sliced water chestnuts, drained
- 2 teaspoons cornstarch mixed with 2 teaspoons cold water

Heat oil in wok until hot. Add beef; stir-fry 1 minute. Add next 4 ingredients; stir-fry 1 minute. Stir cornstarch mixture; add to wok; stir-fry until sauce thickens slightly. Serve immediately.

Note: Cook round steak quickly over high heat or it will toughen.

Stir-Fried Beef and Onions

Makes 2 servings
Preparation Time: 10 minutes; 4 minutes to cook

- 1 tablespoon cornstarch
- 2 tablespoons soy sauce
- 4 tablespoons dry sherry
- ½ pound lean flank or sirloin steak, thinly sliced across grain and cut in 1½-inch-long strips
- ½ teaspoon sugar
- ½ teaspoon salt
- 2 tablespoons peanut oil
- 2 medium onions, peeled, sliced and separated into rings

Mix cornstarch, 1 tablespoon soy sauce and 2 tablespoons sherry in bowl. Add meat; stir to coat; set aside to marinate 10 minutes. Stir together remaining soy sauce, remaining sherry, sugar and salt; set aside. Heat oil in wok until hot. Add onions; stir-fry 2 minutes. Add beef and soy sauce mixture; stir-fry 2 minutes. Serve immediately.

Stir-Fried Beef and Pineapple

Makes 4 servings
Preparation Time: 1 hour; 5 minutes to cook

- 2 tablespoons water
- 1 teaspoon baking soda
- 1 pound beef tenderloin, thinly sliced across grain and cut in 1½-inch-long strips
- 1½ tablespoons cornstarch
- 2 tablespoons soy sauce
- ½ teaspoon sesame oil
- 1 tablespoon water
- 2 drops sesame oil
- 1 teaspoon soy sauce
- 2 tablespoons peanut oil
- ½ small red pepper, cored, seeded and cut in thin 1½-inch-long strips
- ½ small green pepper, cored, seeded and cut in thin 1½-inch-long strips
- 2 ¼-inch slices fresh gingerroot, peeled and minced
- 2 small cloves garlic, peeled and minced
- ½ teaspoon sugar
- 1 pineapple, quartered lengthwise through frond, fruit removed and cubed (reserve shells)

Mix water and baking soda; pour over meat; marinate 1 hour. Mix next 3 ingredients; toss with meat. Mix next 3 ingredients; set aside. Heat oil in wok until hot. Add next 5 ingredients; stir-fry 1 minute. Add beef and reserved soy sauce mixture; stir-fry 2 minutes. Add cubed pineapple and heat through. Divide among 4 pineapple shells. Serve immediately.

Oriental Beef with Vegetables

Makes 4 servings
Preparation Time: 15 minutes; 9 minutes to cook

- 1 pound lean flank or sirloin steak, thinly sliced across grain and cut in 1½-inch-long strips
- 2 tablespoons peanut oil
- 2 tablespoons soy sauce
- 2 tablespoons dry sherry
- ½ teaspoon sugar
- 1 clove garlic, peeled and crushed
- ½ teaspoon peeled and finely grated fresh gingerroot
- 2 teaspoons cornstarch
- 2 tablespoons water
- 3 tablespoons peanut oil
- 1 small onion, peeled, halved and thinly sliced
- 1 small green pepper, cored, seeded and cut in thin 1½-inch long strips
- 1 small red pepper, cored, seeded and cut in thin 1½-inch-long strips
- ½ cup sliced bamboo shoots, drained

Put meat in shallow dish with next 8 ingredients; mix to coat meat. Heat 2 tablespoons oil in wok until hot. Add remaining ingredients; stir-fry 3 to 5 minutes or until vegetables are tender-crisp. Remove from wok; set aside. Wipe out wok with paper towel. Heat remaining 1 tablespoon oil in wok until hot. Add meat; stir-fry 2 minutes or until no longer pink. Return vegetables to wok; stir-fry to heat through. Serve immediately.

Beef and Snow Peas

Makes 3 servings
Preparation Time: 15 minutes; 3 minutes to cook

- ¼ cup soy sauce
- 1 tablespoon cornstarch
- 1 tablespoon dry sherry
- 1 teaspoon sugar
- 1 pound flank or sirloin steak, fat trimmed, thinly sliced across grain and cut in 1½-inch-long strips
- 2 tablespoons peanut oil
- ½ teaspoon salt
- 20 snow peas, ends and strings removed
- ½ cup sliced water chestnuts, drained

Mix first 4 ingredients in bowl. Add meat; stir to coat; marinate 15 minutes. Heat oil in wok until hot. Add meat; stir-fry 2 minutes. Add salt, snow peas and water chestnuts; stir-fry 1 minute. Serve immediately.

Beef with Green Peppers and Tomatoes

Makes 4 to 6 servings
Preparation Time: 15 minutes; 12 minutes to cook

- 2 tablespoons peanut oil
- 1 clove garlic, peeled and crushed
- ½ teaspoon salt
- ½ teaspoon freshly ground black pepper
- ½ teaspoon peeled and minced fresh gingerroot
- 1 pound round steak, fat trimmed, thinly sliced and cut in 1½-inch-long strips
- ¼ cup soy sauce
- ½ teaspoon sugar
- 2 green peppers, cored, seeded and cut in thin 1½-inch-long strips
- 2 tomatoes, cored and quartered
- 3 tablespoons cornstarch mixed with
  ¼ cup cold water
  Hot cooked rice

Heat oil in wok until hot. Add garlic, salt, pepper and gingerroot; stir-fry 3 seconds. Add beef; stir-fry 2 minutes. Add soy sauce, sugar, green peppers; cover; cook 3 minutes. Add tomatoes; cover; cook 2 minutes. Add cornstarch mixture; stir-fry until sauce thickens slightly. Serve immediately with hot cooked rice.

Pork

Mo Shu Pork

Makes 4 servings
Preparation Time: 20 minutes; 4 minutes to cook

- 4 tablespoons peanut oil
- 3 eggs, lightly beaten
- ½ pound pork butt, fat trimmed and cut into thin 1½-inch-long strips
- 1 cup sliced bamboo shoots, drained and thinly sliced into strips
- 10 Chinese dried black mushrooms, soaked in hot water 20 minutes, drained, squeezed dry, stems discarded and caps thinly sliced
- 1 tablespoon soy sauce
- 2 green onions, diagonally cut in ½-inch pieces
- 8 to 10 prepared Chinese Pancakes (Recipe on page 9)
  Duck sauce, optional

Heat 2 tablespoons oil in wok until hot. Add eggs; scramble without overcooking. Turn out onto plate. Heat remaining 2 tablespoons oil in wok until hot. Stir-fry pork 2 minutes. Add bamboo shoots, mushrooms and eggs; stir well, breaking up eggs somewhat. Add soy sauce and green onions; stir-fry 15 seconds. Serve immediately with Chinese Pancakes. Spread some duck sauce on pancakes before filling, if desired. Put a spoonful of pork on a pancake and roll up.

Oriental Pork and Chinese Cabbage

Makes 4 servings
Preparation Time: 10 minutes; 7 minutes to cook

- 3 tablespoons soy sauce
- 1 tablespoon packed light brown sugar
- 1½ teaspoons salt
- ½ teaspoon peeled and minced fresh gingerroot
- 3 tablespoons peanut oil
- 1 pound 1-inch lean pork cubes
- 1 small green pepper, cored, seeded and cut in thin 1-inch-long strips
- 1 small onion, peeled and cut into wedges
- 4 cups loosely packed shredded Chinese cabbage
- ½ cup cold water
- 1 tablespoon cornstarch mixed with 2 teaspoons cold water

Mix first 4 ingredients; set aside. Heat oil in wok until hot. Add pork; stir-fry 3 minutes. Add pepper and onion; stir-fry 1 minute. Add soy sauce mixture, cabbage and water; toss to combine; cover; cook 1 minute. Uncover; stir cornstarch mixture; add to wok; stir-fry until slightly thickened. Serve immediately.

Stir-Fried Pork with Cashews

Makes 4 servings
Preparation Time: 15 minutes; 6 minutes to cook

- 2 tablespoons soy sauce
- 1 tablespoon dry sherry
- 1 teaspoon salt
  Pinch sugar
- 2 tablespoons peanut oil
- ½ teaspoon crushed garlic
- 3 green onions including tops, thinly sliced
- 1 pound lean boneless pork, cut in 1½-inch-long thin strips
- ½ cup sliced bamboo shoots, drained
- ½ cup sliced water chestnuts, drained
- 1 cup fresh bean sprouts
- 2 teaspoons cornstarch mixed with 2 teaspoons cold water
- ⅓ cup unsalted raw cashews

Mix soy sauce, sherry, salt and sugar; set aside. Heat oil in wok until hot. Add garlic and onions; stir-fry 1 minute. Add pork; stir-fry until pinkness is gone, about 3 minutes. Add next 3 ingredients and reserved soy sauce mixture; stir-fry 1 minute. Stir cornstarch mixture; add to wok. Stir-fry until sauce thickens. Add cashews; toss to coat. Serve immediately.

Spicy Pork with Vegetables

Makes 2 servings
Preparation Time: 15 minutes; 6 minutes to cook

- 2 tablespoons black bean sauce
- 1 tablespoon soy sauce
- 1 tablespoon dry sherry
- 2 tablespoons peanut oil
- 1 ¼-inch-thick slice fresh gingerroot, peeled and finely minced
- 2 cloves garlic, peeled and minced
- ¼ teaspoon dried red pepper flakes
- 1 large carrot, pared and very thinly sliced on diagonal
- 1 green pepper, cored, seeded and cut in thin 1½-inch-long strips
- ½ pound thinly sliced 1½-inch-long lean pork strips
- ½ cup sliced bamboo shoots, drained
- ½ cup chicken stock
- 2 teaspoons cornstarch mixed with 2 teaspoons cold water

Mix first 3 ingredients; set aside. Heat oil in wok until hot. Add next 3 ingredients; stir-fry 30 seconds. Add carrot and green pepper; stir-fry 1 minute. Add pork and bean sauce mixture; stir-fry 2 minutes. Add bamboo shoots and stock; cover; cook 1 minute or until carrots are tender-crisp. Uncover; stir cornstarch mixture; add to wok; stir-fry until sauce thickens. Serve immediately.

Spicy Pork with Vegetables, this page

Pork

Pork Strips with Szechwan Sauce

Makes 4 servings
Preparation Time: 15 minutes; 5 minutes to cook

- 1 pound lean boneless pork, cut in thin 1½-inch-long strips
- 1 teaspoon minced garlic
- 4 tablespoons soy sauce
- 1 egg, lightly beaten
- 2 tablespoons cornstarch
- 1 tablespoon dry sherry
- 2 tablespoons vinegar
- ½ cup peanut oil
- ½ teaspoon dried red pepper flakes
- 4 green onions including tops, thinly sliced

Mix pork, ½ teaspoon garlic, 2 tablespoons soy sauce, egg, cornstarch and sherry in bowl; set aside. Mix remaining 2 tablespoons soy sauce and vinegar; set aside. Heat oil in wok until hot. Add pork mixture; stir-fry until pork loses its pinkness, 2 to 3 minutes; remove from wok using strainer; set aside. Drain all but 1 tablespoon oil from wok. Heat until hot. Add red pepper flakes, remaining ½ teaspoon garlic and onions; stir-fry 30 seconds. Return pork to wok with vinegar mixture; stir-fry 1 minute. Serve immediately.

Pork Szechwan

Makes 2 servings
Preparation Time: 15 minutes; 10 minutes to cook

- 1 cup peanut oil
- 1 unpeeled small eggplant, cut in 2-inch cubes
- 2 cloves garlic, peeled and finely chopped
- 2 green onions, tops discarded, thinly sliced
- ¼ teaspoon dried red pepper flakes
- ½ pound lean pork butt, cut in thin 1½-inch-long strips
- 1 teaspoon dry sherry
- 2 teaspoons hot bean sauce
- ½ teaspoon sugar
- ¼ cup chicken stock
- 1 tablespoon vinegar
- ¼ teaspoon sesame oil
- 1 teaspoon cornstarch mixed with 2 tablespoons water

Heat oil in wok until hot. Add eggplant cubes; fry until golden brown, 4 to 5 minutes. Remove with strainer; drain on paper toweling. Pour all but 1 tablespoon oil from wok. Heat oil in wok until hot. Add garlic, onions and red pepper flakes; stir-fry 10 seconds. Add pork; stir-fry until it loses its pinkness. Add sherry and eggplant; stir-fry 10 seconds. Add next 5 ingredients; stir-fry 15 seconds. Stir cornstarch mixture; add to wok. Stir-fry until sauce thickens. Serve immediately.

Sliced Pork with Philippine Sauce

Makes 4 servings.
Preparation Time: 5 minutes; 15 minutes to cook

- 2 tablespoons peanut oil
- 1 small onion, peeled and finely chopped
- 1 clove garlic, peeled and crushed
- 3 tablespoons packed light brown sugar
- ½ cup lime juice
- ½ cup water
- ½ teaspoon peeled and minced fresh gingerroot
- ½ teaspoon salt
  Dash cayenne pepper
- ½ teaspoon cornstarch mixed with 1 tablespoon cold water
  Hot or cold sliced cooked pork roast

Heat oil in wok until hot. Add onion and garlic; stir-fry 1 minute. Add next 6 ingredients; cover; simmer 10 minutes. Stir cornstarch mixture; add to wok and stir. Serve immediately with pork.

Twice-Cooked Pork with Spicy Vegetables

Makes 2 small servings
Preparation Time: 1 hour; 5 minutes to cook

- ½ pound pork butt
- 6 Chinese dried black mushrooms, soaked in hot water 20 minutes, drained (reserve water), stems discarded and caps thinly sliced
- 1 tablespoon soy sauce
  Pinch sugar
- 1 teaspoon salt
- 2 tablespoons peanut oil
- 2 cloves garlic, peeled and minced
- 1 teaspoon peeled and minced fresh gingerroot
- ⅛ teaspoon dried red pepper flakes
- 1 small green pepper, cored, seeded and cut in thin 1-inch-long strips
- 1 large carrot, pared and cut in thin diagonal slices
- ¼ cup sliced bamboo shoots, drained
- 1 teaspoon cornstarch mixed with 1 teaspoon cold water

Cover pork with water in wok; simmer 30 minutes, adding more hot water if level goes below pork. Cool pork in cooking liquid. Remove; cut in thin 1-inch-long strips; set aside. Mix ⅓ cup mushroom water with soy sauce, sugar and salt; set aside. Heat oil in wok until hot. Add garlic, gingerroot, red pepper flakes and mushrooms; stir-fry 30 seconds. Add next 3 ingredients and pork strips; stir-fry 1 minute. Add mushroom liquid mixture; cover; cook 2 minutes. Stir cornstarch mixture; add to wok; stir-fry until sauce thickens. Serve immediately.

Pork

Pork Cubes in Hot Bean-Paste Sauce

Makes 4 servings
Preparation Time: 20 minutes; 6 minutes to cook

- 1 pound ½-inch cubes lean pork
- 2 teaspoons soy sauce
- 2½ teaspoons cornstarch
- 1 small egg, lightly beaten
- 2 tablespoons soy sauce
- 1 teaspoon minced fresh garlic
- 1 teaspoon peeled and minced fresh gingerroot
- 1 tablespoon sugar
- 1 tablespoon water
- 1 tablespoon vinegar
- ½ cup peanut oil
- 10 Chinese dried black mushrooms, soaked in hot water 10 minutes, drained, stems discarded and caps thinly sliced
- ¼ cup sliced water chestnuts, drained
- 1 teaspoon hot bean paste
- 1 green onion including top, thinly sliced
- ½ teaspoon sesame oil

Mix pork, 2 teaspoons soy sauce, cornstarch and egg; set aside. Mix 2 tablespoons soy sauce, garlic, gingerroot, sugar, water and vinegar; set aside. Heat oil in wok until hot. Add pork mixture, mushrooms and water chestnuts; stir-fry until pork loses pinkness, about 3 minutes. Remove pork, mushrooms and water chestnuts with strainer. Pour off all but 1 tablespoon oil. Heat oil until hot. Add bean paste and meat mixture; stir-fry 30 seconds. Add reserved soy sauce mixture and green onions; stir-fry 10 seconds. Stir in sesame oil. Serve immediately.

Pork Stir-Fry

Makes 4 servings
Preparation Time: 10 minutes; 7 minutes to cook

- 2 tablespoons peanut oil
- 2 medium onions, peeled and thinly sliced
- 1 10-inch celery rib, thinly sliced
- 2 cloves garlic, peeled and crushed
- 1 pound thin 1½-inch-long lean pork strips
- ¼ cup chicken stock
- 2 tablespoons dry sherry
- ½ teaspoon salt
  Freshly ground black pepper to taste
- 2 teaspoons cornstarch mixed with
  2 teaspoons cold water
- 2 tablespoons soy sauce

Heat oil in wok until hot. Add onions and celery; stir-fry 2 minutes or until tender-crisp. Add garlic and pork; stir-fry until pork loses its pinkness, 2 to 3 minutes. Add next 4 ingredients; stir-fry 30 seconds. Stir cornstarch mixture; add to wok with soy sauce; stir-fry until sauce thickens. Serve immediately.

Mandarin Ham Stir-Fry

Makes 4 servings
Preparation Time: 10 minutes; 7 minutes to cook

- ¾ cup packed light brown sugar
- ¼ teaspoon dry mustard
- 1 tablespoon cornstarch
- 1 teaspoon peeled and minced fresh gingerroot
- ¼ teaspoon ground cloves
- 1 small clove garlic, peeled and crushed
- ¼ cup vinegar
- ½ cup water
- 2 cups 1-inch ham cubes

Mix all ingredients except ham in wok. Heat; cook 5 minutes. Add ham; stir-fry to heat ham through. Serve immediately.

Pork and Vegetables with Almonds

Makes 4 servings
Preparation Time: 10 minutes; 12 minutes to cook

- 1 teaspoon peanut oil
- ½ cup slivered blanched almonds
- 1 pound lean pork, cut in ½-inch cubes
- 1 egg white, lightly beaten
- 4 tablespoons cornstarch
- ½ teaspoon salt
- 2 tablespoons dry sherry
- 1¼ cups chicken stock
- 2 tablespoons peanut oil
- 1 teaspoon peeled and minced fresh gingerroot
- 1 cup thinly sliced carrot
- 1 small green pepper, cored, seeded and cut into thin 1½-inch-long strips
- 1 8-ounce can sliced water chestnuts, drained
  Slivered blanched almonds, for garnish

Heat 1 teaspoon oil in wok until hot. Add almonds; stir-fry until evenly browned. Remove with strainer; drain thoroughly on paper towel; set aside. Toss pork with egg white, 2 tablespoons cornstarch and salt to thoroughly coat; set aside. Mix remaining 2 tablespoons cornstarch, sherry and ¼ cup chicken stock; set aside. Heat 2 tablespoons oil in wok until hot. Add pork mixture; stir-fry until pork loses pinkness, 2 to 3 minutes. Add gingerroot, remaining 1 cup chicken stock and carrot; cover; cook 5 minutes or until carrot is tender. Uncover; add green pepper; cover; cook 2 minutes. Add water chestnuts. Stir cornstarch mixture; add to wok; stir-fry until sauce thickens. Sprinkle with almonds. Serve immediately.

Pork with Green Onions and Water Chestnuts

Makes 4 servings
Preparation Time: 15 minutes; 5 minutes to cook

    4 tablespoons soy sauce
    2 tablespoons cold water
    4 teaspoons cornstarch
    1 teaspoon sugar
    1½ pounds boneless lean pork, cut in 2 x 2 x ⅛-inch
      slices
    2 tablespoons dry sherry
    2 teaspoons rice vinegar
    1 teaspoon sesame oil
    2 tablespoons peanut oil
    2 cloves garlic, peeled and finely minced
    4 green onions including tops, cut in
      ½-inch-long slices
    ½ cup sliced bamboo shoots, drained

Mix 2 tablespoons soy sauce, cold water, cornstarch and sugar in bowl; add pork; set aside 15 minutes. Mix remaining 2 tablespoons soy sauce, sherry, vinegar and sesame oil; set aside. Heat oil in wok over high heat until hot. Add garlic; stir-fry 10 seconds. Add pork; stir-fry 3 minutes. Add onions and bamboo shoots; stir-fry 30 seconds. Add sherry mixture; stir until smooth. Serve immediately.

Pork and Straw Mushroom Stir-Fry

Makes 4 servings
Preparation Time: 30 minutes; 7 minutes to cook

    1 tablespoon cornstarch
    ½ teaspoon salt
    ½ teaspoon sugar
    1 pound lean pork, cut in ½-inch cubes
    2 tablespoons soy sauce
    1 tablespoon dry sherry
    4 tablespoons peanut oil
    1 teaspoon peeled and minced fresh gingerroot
    2 to 3 thin carrots, pared and sliced diagonally ⅛ inch
      thick
    1 15-ounce can baby ears of corn, drained and rinsed
    ¼ cup chicken stock
    1 15-ounce can straw mushrooms, drained and rinsed
    ¼ pound snow peas, ends and strings removed

Mix first 3 ingredients in bowl; add meat; toss to coat well. Add soy sauce and wine; toss again; marinate 30 minutes. Heat 2 tablespoons oil in wok until hot. Add pork; stir-fry until pinkness is gone; remove with strainer; set aside. Remove oil; wipe wok with paper towel. Heat remaining 2 tablespoons oil in wok until hot. Add gingerroot and carrots; stir-fry 2 minutes. Add corn; stir-fry 10 seconds. Return pork mixture to wok with stock; stir. Add mushrooms and snow peas; stir-fry 30 seconds. Serve immediately.

Sweet and Sour Pork

Makes 6 servings
Preparation Time: 20 minutes; 15 minutes to cook

    2 pounds boneless pork loin, cut in ½-inch cubes
    ¼ cup soy sauce
    1 egg, lightly beaten
      Cornstarch
      Vegetable oil
    1 large onion, peeled and cut in 8 wedges
    1 green pepper, cored, seeded and
      cut in 1-inch pieces
    1 cup pineapple chunks, drained and juice reserved
    2 small tomatoes, cored and cut in wedges
      Sweet and Sour Sauce

Toss pork with soy sauce; roll in egg; roll in cornstarch, shaking off excess cornstarch. Heat oil in wok until hot. Add pork in batches, stir-frying until golden brown. Drain on paper towels; keep warm in preheated 200° oven. Drain all but 1 tablespoon oil from wok; heat until hot. Add onion; stir-fry 2 minutes. Add green pepper; stir-fry 2 minutes. Add pineapple and tomatoes; stir-fry 1 minute. Return pork to wok; add Sweet and Sour Sauce; stir-fry to coat all ingredients with sauce. Serve immediately.

Sweet and Sour Sauce

    ½ cup reserved pineapple juice
    ½ cup white wine vinegar
    2 tablespoons peanut oil
    2 tablespoons packed light brown sugar
    1 tablespoon soy sauce
    ½ teaspoon freshly ground black pepper
    2 teaspoons cornstarch mixed with
      4 teaspoons cold water

Mix first 6 ingredients in wok; bring to boil. Stir cornstarch mixture; add to wok, stirring until sauce is clear and slightly thickened.

Sweet and Sour Pork, this page;
Pork and Straw Mushroom Stir-Fry, this page

Chicken

Stir-Fried Chicken and Vegetables

Makes 4 servings
Preparation Time: 15 minutes; 5 minutes to cook

- ½ cup cold water
- 2 teaspoons cornstarch
- ½ teaspoon peeled and finely minced fresh gingerroot
- 2 teaspoons soy sauce
- 2 tablespoons peanut oil
- 1 medium onion, peeled, halved and sliced
- 1 teaspoon minced garlic
- 1 whole chicken breast, split, skinned, boned and cut in ¾-inch pieces
- 1 green pepper, cored, seeded and cut in thin 1½-inch-long strips
- 2 tomatoes, cored and each cut in 6 wedges

Mix water, cornstarch, gingerroot and soy sauce; set aside. Heat oil in wok until hot. Add onion and garlic; stir-fry 1 minute. Add chicken and green pepper; stir-fry 3 minutes. Add tomatoes; stir-fry 1 minute. Stir cornstarch mixture; add to wok; cook until sauce thickens. Serve immediately.

Szechwan Chicken

Makes 4 servings
Preparation Time: 15 minutes; 6 minutes to cook

- 1 tablespoon cornstarch
- 3 tablespoons soy sauce
- 2 whole chicken breasts, split, skinned, boned and cut in ½-inch cubes
- 1 tablespoon dry sherry
- 2 teaspoons sugar
- 1 teaspoon vinegar
- ¼ cup peanut oil
- ½ to 1 teaspoon dried red pepper flakes
- 2 green onions including tops, sliced
- ½ teaspoon peeled and minced fresh gingerroot
- ½ cup dry-roasted peanuts
  Hot cooked rice

Blend cornstarch and 1 tablespoon soy sauce in bowl. Mix in chicken; set aside. Mix remaining 2 tablespoons soy sauce, sherry, sugar and vinegar; set aside. Heat oil in wok over high heat. When hot, add red pepper flakes; stir-fry until black, 10 seconds. Add chicken; stir-fry 2 minutes. Remove chicken with strainer; set aside. Add green onions and gingerroot; stir-fry 1 minute. Add chicken; stir-fry 2 minutes. Add sherry mixture; stir-fry 1 minute. Stir in peanuts. Serve with hot rice.

Stir-Fried Chicken and Broccoli

Makes 4 servings
Preparation Time: 15 minutes; 10 minutes to cook

- 1 whole chicken breast, split, skinned, boned and thinly sliced
- 3 tablespoons cornstarch
- ¼ cup soy sauce
- 2 tablespoons peanut oil
- ½ pound broccoli, cut in small pieces
- 1 medium onion, peeled and thinly sliced
- ¼ pound mushrooms, wiped clean and sliced
- 2 cups fresh bean sprouts
- 1 cup hot chicken stock

Stir first 3 ingredients in bowl until chicken is thoroughly coated; set aside 15 minutes. Heat 1 tablespoon oil in wok until hot. Add chicken; stir-fry 3 minutes; remove from wok with strainer. Add 1 tablespoon oil to wok; heat until hot. Add broccoli and onion; stir-fry 2 minutes. Add mushrooms, bean sprouts, chicken and stock; cover; cook 5 minutes or until vegetables are tender-crisp. Serve immediately.

Walnut Chicken

Makes 4 servings
Preparation Time: 20 minutes; 8 minutes to cook

- ½ cup water
- 2 tablespoons cornstarch
- 1 tablespoon soy sauce
- ½ teaspoon sugar
- ½ teaspoon salt
- 3 tablespoons peanut oil
- 1 cup walnut halves
- 1 whole chicken breast, split, skinned, boned and slivered
- 6 Chinese dried black mushrooms, soaked in hot water 20 minutes, drained, stems discarded, caps quartered
- 12 snow peas, ends and strings removed
- 6 fresh mushrooms, wiped clean and sliced
- ½ cup sliced water chestnuts, drained
- ½ cup sliced bamboo shoots, drained

Mix first 5 ingredients; set aside. Heat 1 tablespoon oil in wok; add walnuts; stir-fry 1 minute. Do not let burn. Remove walnuts with strainer; drain on paper towel. Discard oil in wok. Heat remaining 2 tablespoons oil in wok until hot. Add chicken; stir-fry 3 minutes. Add next 5 ingredients; stir-fry 3 minutes. Add cornstarch mixture; cook until thickened. Serve immediately topped with walnuts.

Chicken with Button Mushrooms

Makes 2 servings
Preparation Time: 10 minutes; 7 minutes to cook

- **1 teaspoon cornstarch mixed with**
  1 teaspoon cold water
- **1 tablespoon dry sherry**
- **1 tablespoon oyster sauce**
- **1 teaspoon water**
- **½ teaspoon salt**
- **1 whole chicken breast, split, skinned, boned and cubed**
- **2 teaspoons dry white wine** *or* **dry vermouth**
- **1 egg white, lightly beaten**
- **1 teaspoon cornstarch**
  Salt and freshly ground white pepper to taste
- **2 tablespoons peanut oil**
- **¼ pound snow peas, ends and strings removed**
- **¼ cup sliced water chestnuts, drained**
- **¼ cup sliced bamboo shoots, drained**
- **24 fresh button mushrooms**

Stir cornstarch mixture; add next 4 ingredients; mix well; set aside. Mix next 4 ingredients; season with salt and pepper. Heat oil in wok until hot. Add chicken; stir-fry until opaque. Add snow peas, water chestnuts, bamboo shoots and mushrooms; stir-fry 3 minutes. Stir sherry mixture; add to wok. Cook, stirring, 1 minute. Serve immediately.

Spiced Orange Chicken

Makes 4 servings
Preparation Time: 15 minutes; 6 to 7 minutes to cook

- **2 whole chicken breasts, split, skinned, boned and cut in 1-inch cubes**
- **1 teaspoon salt**
- **1 egg, lightly beaten**
- **2 tablespoons cornstarch**
- **5 tablespoons peanut oil, divided**
- **2 tablespoons soy sauce**
- **1 tablespoon sugar**
- **1 teaspoon sesame oil**
- **1 tablespoon dry sherry**
- **1 teaspoon white vinegar**
  Grated peel from 2 tangerines
- **¼ teaspoon dried red pepper flakes**
- **4 ¼-inch slices fresh gingerroot, peeled and coarsely chopped**
- **3 to 4 green onions, cut diagonally in ¼-inch slices**

Mix chicken, salt, egg, 1 tablespoon cornstarch and 1 tablespoon oil in bowl until chicken is coated; set aside. Mix next 5 ingredients and remaining 1 tablespoon cornstarch; set aside. Heat 3 tablespoons oil in wok until hot. Stir-fry chicken until opaque, about 3 minutes. Remove with strainer; set aside. Heat 1 tablespoon oil in wok until hot; add tangerine peel and red pepper flakes. Cook until blackened, about 10 seconds, stirring constantly. Add gingerroot, green onions and chicken; stir-fry 10 seconds. Stir soy mixture; add to wok; stir-fry 1 minute. Serve immediately.

Chicken with Oyster Sauce

Makes 4 servings
Preparation Time: 15 minutes; 6 minutes to cook

- **1 tablespoon soy sauce**
- **½ teaspoon sugar**
- **½ teaspoon salt**
- **1 tablespoon oyster sauce**
- **2 tablespoons peanut oil**
- **1 clove garlic, peeled and split**
- **1 large green pepper, cored, seeded and cut in 1-inch pieces**
- **1 onion, peeled and cut in 1-inch cubes**
- **2 whole chicken breasts, split, skinned, boned and cut in 1-inch cubes**

Mix soy sauce, sugar, salt and oyster sauce; set aside. Heat oil in wok until hot. Swirl garlic around sides and bottom of wok about 30 seconds; discard. Add pepper and onion; stir-fry 1 minute. Add chicken; stir-fry 3 minutes or until opaque. Add soy sauce mixture; stir well. Serve immediately.

Chicken with Hoisin Sauce and Nuts

Makes 4 servings
Preparation Time: 20 minutes; 7 minutes to cook

- **1 tablespoon cornstarch**
- **2 tablespoons dry sherry**
- **2 whole chicken breasts, split, skinned, boned and cut into 1-inch cubes**
- **3 tablespoons peanut oil**
- **6 large Chinese dried black mushrooms, soaked in hot water 20 minutes, drained, stems discarded, caps quartered**
- **1 small green pepper, cored, seeded and cut in thin 1½-inch-long strips**
- **½ cup sliced water chestnuts, drained**
- **½ teaspoon salt**
- **1 tablespoon sugar mixed with**
  3 tablespoons hoisin sauce
- **¼ cup unsalted raw cashews, almonds, pecans** *or* **peanuts**

Mix cornstarch and sherry in bowl; add chicken; stir; set aside. Heat 1 tablespoon oil in wok until hot; add mushrooms; stir-fry 1 minute. Add pepper and water chestnuts; stir-fry 1 minute. Add salt; mix. Remove vegetables from wok with strainer; set aside. Add remaining 2 tablespoons oil to wok; heat until hot. Add chicken; stir-fry 3 minutes or until opaque. Add sugar-hoisin mixture; toss well. Return vegetables to wok; mix. Add nuts; mix. Serve immediately.

Hot Shredded Chicken

Makes 2 servings
Preparation Time: 1 hour, 15 minutes

  3 chicken thighs
  4 teaspoons dry mustard
  ¼ cup cold water
  1 cup peanut oil
  2 ounces rice sticks, pulled apart slightly
  ½ teaspoon five-spice powder
  ½ teaspoon salt
  3 tablespoons soy sauce
  4 teaspoons sesame seed oil
  6 to 8 green onions including 2-inches of tops, cut in
    3-inch lengths, then cut lengthwise in thin strips

Put chicken on rack over boiling water in wok. Cover; steam 1 hour, adding boiling water if needed. Blend mustard with water; let stand 15 to 20 minutes. Heat oil in wok until hot. Add chicken thighs; fry until crisp, 5 to 8 minutes. Drain on paper towels; cool; cut meat in thin lengthwise strips. Add rice sticks to oil heated to 325°. Sticks will puff immediately; turn with tongs; cook 30 seconds on other side. Remove to paper towels to drain; place on platter. Blend five-spice powder, salt, soy sauce and sesame seed oil into mustard mixture. Add onions and chicken; toss to coat. Spoon mixture over rice sticks. Serve within 30 minutes.

Shredded Chicken Hunan-Style

Makes 4 servings
Preparation Time: 15 minutes; 3 to 4 minutes to cook

  ⅓ cup dry sherry
  ¼ teaspoon salt
  ¼ teaspoon sugar
  ¼ cup chicken stock
  4 green onions including tops, cut in ½-inch pieces
  2 ¼-inch slices fresh gingerroot, peeled and diced
  1 tablespoon cornstarch mixed with
    2 tablespoons cold water
  1 whole chicken breast, split, skinned, boned and cut
    in ⅛-inch-thick slices
  2 egg whites
  ½ teaspoon salt
  2 tablespoons dry sherry
  3 tablespoons cornstarch
  1½ cups peanut oil
  12 snow peas, ends and strings removed
  2 cups fresh bean sprouts

Mix ⅓ cup dry sherry and next 6 ingredients; set aside. Put chicken shreds in bowl with next 3 ingredients; mix with fork vigorously until chicken is coated. Add cornstarch; mix with fork until smooth. Heat oil in wok to 280°. Add chicken mixture; stir-fry 1 minute, breaking up chicken with spatula. Remove chicken with strainer; pour all but 1 tablespoon oil from wok; heat oil in wok until hot. Add snow peas and bean sprouts; stir-fry 15 seconds. Return chicken to wok; add sherry mixture; cook until sauce is thickened. Serve immediately.

Note: Slicing chicken is easier when chicken is partially frozen.

Chicken with Cashews and Snow Peas

Makes 2 servings
Preparation Time: 15 minutes; 5 minutes to cook

  1 whole chicken breast, split, skinned, boned and cut
    in 1-inch cubes
  2 cloves garlic, peeled and minced
  1 tablespoon soy sauce
  1 tablespoon dry sherry
  2 tablespoons cornstarch
  1 teaspoon hoisin sauce
  1 tablespoon peanut oil
  20 snow peas, ends and strings removed
  ½ cup sliced water chestnuts, drained
  ½ cup hot chicken stock
  ½ teaspoon salt
  ½ cup unsalted raw cashews

Marinate chicken 15 minutes in mixture of next 5 ingredients. Heat oil in wok until hot. Add chicken mixture; stir-fry 3 minutes. Add snow peas and water chestnuts; stir-fry 30 seconds. Add stock and salt; stir-fry until slightly thickened. Stir in cashews. Serve immediately.

Chicken Livers Chinese-Style

Makes 4 servings
Preparation Time: 10 minutes; 10 minutes to cook

  2 tablespoons soy sauce
  2 tablespoons water
  1 tablespoon cornstarch
  3 slices bacon
  1 pound chicken livers, fat trimmed, each cut in
    3 pieces
  4 green onions including tops, chopped
  1 medium green pepper, cored, seeded and chopped

Mix first 3 ingredients; set aside. Fry bacon in wok until crisp; drain; crumble; set aside. Brown livers and onions in fat in wok, about 3 minutes. Near end of browning, add green pepper. Stir soy mixture; add to wok. Stir until sauce thickens slightly. Stir in reserved bacon. Serve immediately.

Chicken with Cashews and Snow Peas,
this page

Chicken

Almond Chicken

Makes 4 servings
Preparation Time: 15 minutes; 7 minutes to cook

    2 tablespoons peanut oil
    1 whole chicken breast, split, skinned, boned and
        thinly sliced
    ½ cup sliced bamboo shoots, drained
    ½ teaspoon salt
    ½ cup sliced water chestnuts, drained
    ½ cup slivered almonds
    2 tablespoons soy sauce
    1 cup chicken stock
    3 tablespoons cornstarch mixed with
        ½ cup cold water

Heat oil in wok until hot. Add chicken; stir-fry 3 minutes or until chicken is opaque. Add next 6 ingredients; cover; cook 3 minutes. Stir cornstarch mixture; add to wok. Stir-fry until slightly thickened. Serve immediately.

Chicken Delicious

Makes 4 servings
Preparation Time: 20 minutes; 4 minutes to cook

    2 whole chicken breasts, split, skinned, boned and
        cut in 1-inch cubes
    1 tablespoon cornstarch
    1 tablespoon dry sherry
    1 tablespoon soy sauce
    2 tablespoons peanut oil
    ¼ pound fresh mushrooms, wiped clean and sliced
    1 green pepper, cored, seeded and
        cut in 1-inch pieces
    1 heaping tablespoon hoisin sauce
        Salt to taste
    ⅓ cup unsalted raw cashews

Sprinkle chicken with cornstarch; toss to coat thoroughly. Add sherry and soy sauce; marinate 15 minutes at room temperature. Heat oil in wok until hot. Add chicken; stir-fry 3 minutes. Add mushrooms and green pepper; stir-fry 45 seconds. Add remaining ingredients; toss to mix. Serve immediately.

Lemon Chicken

Makes 2 to 4 servings
Preparation Time: 40 minutes

    1 chicken
        Chicken stock
        Juice of 3 lemons
    ½ cup sugar
    ½ cup boiling water

Simmer chicken in chicken stock to cover in wok until nearly tender, about 20 minutes. Remove;

halve lengthwise; place on broiler rack. Broil 4 to 5 inches from heat 10 minutes; turn; broil another 10 minutes or until golden brown. Meanwhile, mix lemon juice, sugar and boiling water in saucepan. Bring to boil; simmer 2 to 3 minutes. Remove from heat; set aside. Arrange chicken halves on platter; spoon lemon sauce over chicken.

Chinese Chicken and Shrimp Salad

Makes 6 servings
Preparation Time: 20 minutes

        Peanut oil
    6 ounces rice sticks
    2 whole chicken breasts, cooked, skinned, boned and
        shredded
    ½ pound medium shrimp, shelled, deveined and
        cooked
    1 cup thinly sliced celery
    1 cup slivered almonds
    1 large zucchini, cut in 2-inch-long julienne strips
    1 head iceberg lettuce, shredded
    1 cup thinly sliced red radishes
    1 cup chopped green onions
        Dressing

Heat at least 1½ cups oil in wok to 375°. Drop rice sticks, 1 ounce at a time, into oil. After they puff (about 30 seconds), remove immediately. Do not brown. Drain on paper towels. Cool; store in airtight container until serving time. To serve, toss rice sticks, chicken, shrimp, celery, almonds and zucchini in bowl. Toss remaining ingredients except Dressing in large bowl; top with ingredients in other bowl; toss. Add desired amount of Dressing; toss. Serve immediately.

Dressing

Makes approximately 1¼ cups.

    2 tablespoons sesame oil
    ¼ cup peanut oil
    ½ cup cider vinegar
    ¼ cup soy sauce
    ½ teaspoon sugar
    1 teaspoon five-spice powder
    1 clove garlic, peeled and minced
    2 tablespoons toasted sesame seed

Place all ingredients in jar with tight-fitting lid; let stand at room temperature at least 1 hour to blend flavors. Shake before serving.

Steamed Chicken with Vegetables

Makes 4 servings
Preparation Time: 20 minutes; 45 minutes to cook

    1 chicken, cut into serving pieces
    2 unpeeled zucchini, cut in thick diagonal slices
    2 large carrots, pared and cut in thick diagonal slices
    2 potatoes, peeled and sliced diagonally
    1 large rib celery, sliced diagonally
    2 sprigs parsley
  ½ teaspoon dried tarragon
    1 bay leaf
      Salt to taste
      Sauce

Place chicken pieces on steamer rack in wok. Top with next 7 ingredients. Season with salt. Cover; steam over hot water 45 minutes or until chicken and vegetables are tender. Remove bay leaf. Serve with Sauce.

Sauce

Makes approximately 1 cup

    1 cup dry white wine *or* dry vermouth
    1 shallot, peeled and minced
    1 tablespoon unsalted butter
    1 cup chicken stock
      Freshly ground white pepper to taste

Boil wine in wok until reduced by half. In another wok or saucepan, sauté shallot in butter 4 to 5 minutes over low to medium heat. Do not brown. Add to wok with stock; cook until reduced by one-third. Season with pepper.

Eight Delicious Chicken

Makes 4 servings
Preparation Time: 20 minutes; 10 minutes to cook

1½ cups peanut *or* vegetable oil
    1 whole chicken breast, split, skinned, boned and cut into ½-inch cubes
  ½ cup small shelled shrimp
    1 tablespoon peeled and diced fresh gingerroot
    1 clove garlic, peeled and finely chopped
  ¼ cup sliced bamboo shoots, drained
  ¼ cup sliced water chestnuts, drained
    6 canned Chinese baby corn, drained
  ½ cup button mushrooms
    8 to 10 Chinese dried black mushrooms, soaked in hot water 20 minutes, drained, stems discarded, caps quartered
    2 tablespoons dry sherry
    1 tablespoon sugar
    3 tablespoons soy sauce
    2 teaspoons hoisin sauce
  ½ cup unsalted peanuts

Heat oil in wok to 325°. Add chicken; stir-fry 3 minutes. Add shrimp; stir-fry until pink. Remove chicken and shrimp with strainer; set aside. Drain all but 2 tablespoons oil from wok. (Oil can be reserved for future use.) Increase heat; add gingerroot and garlic; stir-fry 10 seconds. Add bamboo shoots, water chestnuts, baby corn, button and black mushrooms; stir-fry until vegetables are tender-crisp, about 3 minutes. Mix sherry, sugar, soy and hoisin sauce; pour over vegetables. Add chicken and shrimp; stir-fry 2 minutes. Add peanuts; stir. Serve immediately.

Crisp Chicken Salad

Makes 4 servings
Preparation Time: 20 minutes; 3 hours to marinate

    2 whole chicken breasts, split, skinned and boned
1½ cups chicken stock
  ½ cup sliced green onions
  ½ cup sliced water chestnuts, drained
  ¼ cup sesame seed, lightly toasted
  ¼ pound snow peas, ends and strings removed, cut in julienne strips
      Dressing
      Salt and freshly ground black pepper to taste

Simmer chicken breasts in chicken stock 15 minutes. Let cool in broth; remove; cut meat in ¼-inch strips. Mix chicken, green onions, water chestnuts, sesame seed and snow peas in large bowl. Toss with enough Dressing to coat ingredients. Season with salt and pepper. Serve immediately.

Dressing

Makes 1 cup

    1 ¼-inch slice fresh gingerroot, peeled
    2 tablespoons dry sherry
    1 egg yolk
    1 tablespoon Dijon mustard
1½ teaspoons fresh lemon juice
  ½ cup peanut oil *or* ¼ cup peanut oil and ¼ cup olive oil
    1 tablespoon soy sauce
      Salt and freshly ground white pepper to taste

Marinate gingerroot in sherry 3 hours. Beat yolk with mustard. Add lemon juice; beat to combine. Add oil in thin stream, whisking constantly until thickened and smooth. Remove gingerroot from sherry; add soy sauce, whisking constantly. Season with salt and pepper.

Fish and Seafood

Jade Fish

Makes 4 servings
Preparation Time: 15 minutes; 20 minutes to cook

> 1 2-pound bass *or* red snapper, cleaned, head and tail
>   intact *or* 1-inch-thick fillets
>   Hot water
>   Lettuce leaves
> ¼ cup peanut oil
> 20 snow peas, ends and strings removed
> ½ pound sliced fresh mushrooms
> 1½ cups fish stock
> 5 green onions including tops, cut in
>   1½-inch diagonal slices
> 2 teaspoons soy sauce
> 1 tablespoon oyster sauce
> ¼ teaspoon dried red pepper flakes, optional
> 1 teaspoon vinegar
> ½ teaspoon salt
> ½ teaspoon sugar
> 2 tablespoons cornstarch mixed with
>   ¼ cup cold water

Put fish on rack in wok or in steamer basket. Add hot water; cover; steam 10 to 15 minutes or until fish is opaque. Meanwhile, line deep platter with lettuce leaves. Carefully lift fish from water using slotted spatula; place on lettuce. Clean wok. Heat oil in wok until hot. Add snow peas; stir-fry 30 seconds; remove with strainer; set aside. Add mushrooms; stir-fry 1 minute. Add next 8 ingredients; bring to boil. Stir cornstarch mixture; add to wok; stir until slightly thickened. Add snow peas; reheat. Arrange snow peas around fish; pour sauce over all. Serve immediately.

Oriental Scallops

Makes 6 servings
Preparation Time: 10 minutes; 5 minutes to cook

> ¼ cup cold water
> 2 tablespoons cornstarch
> 1 tablespoon soy sauce
> ½ teaspoon salt
> ⅛ teaspoon freshly ground white pepper
> 2 tablespoons peanut oil
> 2 pounds scallops, halved if large
> 30 snow peas, ends and strings removed
> 2 medium tomatoes, cored and each cut into
>   6 wedges

Mix first 5 ingredients; set aside. Heat oil in wok until hot. Add scallops; stir-fry 2 to 3 minutes until opaque. Add snow peas and tomatoes; stir-fry 1 minute. Stir cornstarch mixture; add to wok. Stir until thickened. Serve immediately.

Poor Man's Lobster

Makes 6 servings
Preparation Time: 20 minutes

> 2 pounds cod fillets
>   Water
> 1 teaspoon salt
> 1 bay leaf
> 1 small onion, peeled and sliced
> 1 slice lemon
> ½ cup dry vermouth
>   Hot melted butter
>   Chopped fresh parsley

Place fish in wok. Cover with water and next 5 ingredients; bring to boil. Reduce heat; simmer 8 to 10 minutes or until fish is opaque. Carefully remove fish from wok with slotted spatula. Serve hot with melted butter and chopped parsley.

Shrimp and Vegetable Stir-Fry

Makes 6 servings
Preparation Time: 15 minutes; approximately 6 minutes to cook

> 2 tablespoons peanut oil
> 2 ¼-inch slices fresh gingerroot,
>   peeled and minced
> 1 clove garlic, peeled and finely chopped
> 1½ cups small broccoli flowerets
> 1½ cups thin diagonal carrot slices
> 1 small onion, peeled and sliced into thin rings
> 1 small green pepper *or* ½ green pepper and ½ red
>   pepper, cored, seeded and cut vertically into thin
>   1½-inch-long strips
> ¾ cup chicken stock
> 1 teaspoon salt
> ½ pound large shrimp, shelled and deveined
> 1 tablespoon cornstarch mixed with
>   2 tablespoons cold water
> 1 8-ounce can sliced water chestnuts, drained
> 1 cup thinly sliced fresh mushrooms
> 2 tablespoons oyster sauce

Heat oil in wok until hot. Add gingerroot and garlic; stir-fry 15 seconds. Add broccoli, carrots, onion and pepper; stir-fry 1 minute. Add chicken stock and salt; toss to combine; cover; cook until carrots are tender-crisp, 2 to 3 minutes. Uncover; add shrimp; stir-fry 1 minute or until pink. Stir cornstarch mixture; add to wok with remaining ingredients; stir-fry 30 to 45 seconds or until heated thoroughly. Serve immediately.

Jade Fish, this page

Fish and Seafood

Shrimp Egg Foo Yung

Makes 4 servings
Preparation Time: 5 minutes; 20 to 30 minutes to cook

> 1 cup fresh bean sprouts
> ½ cup sliced water chestnuts, drained and chopped
> 1 6¼-ounce can small shrimp, drained
> 4 eggs, lightly beaten
> 1 teaspoon salt
> ½ teaspoon freshly ground white pepper
> 3 tablespoons peanut oil
>   Sauce

Mix all ingredients except oil and Sauce in bowl. Heat 1 tablespoon oil in wok until hot. Pour ¼ of mixture into wok; form into round cake; brown on both sides. Remove; keep warm. Brown remaining cakes using remaining oil as needed. Serve immediately with Sauce.

Sauce

> 1½ teaspoons packed light brown sugar
> ¼ cup boiling beef stock
> 1 tablespoon cornstarch mixed with
>   2 tablespoons cold water
> 1 tablespoon soy sauce
> 1 tablespoon dark molasses
>   Pinch freshly ground black pepper

Dissolve brown sugar in beef stock in saucepan. Stir cornstarch mixture; add to saucepan with remaining ingredients; stir over moderate heat until thickened.

Shrimp in Bean Sauce

Makes 4 servings
Preparation Time: 15 minutes; 6 minutes to cook

> 1 tablespoon dry sherry
> 2 teaspoons peeled and minced fresh gingerroot
> 1 tablespoon soy sauce
> ¼ teaspoon freshly ground white pepper
> 1 pound large shrimp, shelled except for tail, deveined
> 4 tablespoons peanut oil
> 1 small onion, peeled, halved and sliced
> 1 cup frozen tiny peas
> ½ small green pepper, cored, seeded and cut in ½-inch-long strips
> ½ small red pepper, cored, seeded and cut in ½-inch-long strips
> 2 cloves garlic, peeled and minced
> 2 tablespoons bean sauce
> 2 teaspoons cornstarch mixed with
>   2 tablespoons cold water

Mix first 4 ingredients; pour over shrimp; marinate 15 minutes; drain. Heat 2 tablespoons oil in wok until hot. Stir-fry next 4 ingredients 2 min-

utes; remove with strainer; set aside. Add remaining 2 tablespoons oil; stir-fry garlic and bean sauce 10 seconds. Add shrimp; stir-fry until pink, about 2 minutes. Return vegetables to wok; stir cornstarch mixture; add to wok. Stir-fry until sauce thickens. Serve immediately.

Steamed Fish Chinois

Makes 4 servings
Preparation Time: 1 hour; 10 to 15 minutes to cook

> 3 tablespoons soy sauce
> ½ cup dry sherry
> 2 tablespoons fresh lemon juice
> 1 clove garlic, peeled and crushed
> 2 pounds halibut, salmon, haddock or cod fillets
>   Water

Mix first 4 ingredients in shallow baking dish. Add fillets; marinate 1 hour. Heat water in wok until simmering. Place fillets in steamer basket or on steamer ring in 1 layer over simmering water. Cover; steam fish until opaque, 10 minutes per 1-inch thickness of fish. Serve immediately.

Fish and Snow Peas

Makes 4 servings
Preparation Time: 15 minutes; 4 minutes to cook

> 1 pound cod fillets, cut in 1 x 3 x ½-inch pieces
> 2 tablespoons cornstarch
> 1 egg white, lightly beaten
> 1 clove garlic, peeled and crushed
> 1 green onion, thinly sliced
> ½ cup sliced water chestnuts, drained
> 20 to 30 snow peas, ends and strings removed
> ¼ cup dry sherry
> 1 teaspoon sugar
> ½ teaspoon salt
> ½ teaspoon sesame oil
> 1 tablespoon cold water
> 2 tablespoons peanut oil

Toss fish, 1 tablespoon cornstarch and egg white in bowl; set aside. Combine garlic and onion; set aside. Combine water chestnuts and snow peas; set aside. Mix next 5 ingredients with remaining 1 tablespoon cornstarch; set aside. Heat 1 tablespoon oil in wok until hot. Add garlic mixture; stir-fry 15 seconds. Add snow pea mixture; stir-fry 30 seconds; remove from wok using strainer; set aside. Heat remaining 1 tablespoon oil in wok until hot. Add fish; gently stir-fry 1 minute. Return vegetables to wok; stir-fry 15 seconds. Stir cornstarch mixture; add to wok. Stir gently until sauce thickens slightly. Serve immediately.

Stir-Fried Shrimp

Makes 4 servings
Preparation Time: 25 minutes; 4½ minutes to cook

- 2 ¼-inch slices fresh gingerroot, peeled
- 1 large clove garlic, peeled
- 2 tablespoons soy sauce
- 1 tablespoon dry sherry
- 2 tablespoons catsup
- 1 teaspoon sugar
- Pinch cayenne pepper
- 2 tablespoons peanut oil
- 1 pound raw shrimp, shelled, deveined and patted dry
- 2 green onions including tops, cut diagonally in 1-inch pieces

Crush gingerroot and garlic together; set aside. Mix next 5 ingredients; set aside. Heat oil in wok until hot. Add gingerroot and garlic; stir-fry 10 seconds. Add shrimp; stir-fry 3 minutes or until pink. Add green onion; stir-fry 30 seconds. Add soy sauce mixture; stir-fry 30 seconds. Serve immediately.

Note: For hotter taste, use ⅛ teaspoon cayenne pepper.

Stir-Fried Smelt with Sauce

Makes 4 servings
Preparation Time: 20 minutes; 15 to 20 minutes to cook

- 1½ pounds smelts, heads, tails and fins removed
- Salt and freshly ground black pepper to taste
- 3 tablespoons fresh lemon juice
- ¼ cup milk
- 1 tablespoon peanut oil
- ½ cup flour
- 1 cup peanut oil
- 4 anchovy fillets, mashed
- 1 tablespoon bread crumbs
- 1 tablespoon chopped fresh parsley

Lay smelts in 1 layer on counter. Season with salt and pepper. Sprinkle with 2 tablespoons lemon juice. Mix milk and 1 tablespoon oil. Dip smelts, one at a time, into milk mixture, then into flour to coat well; set aside. Heat oil in wok until hot. Fry smelts on both sides until brown and crisp; remove with strainer to warm platter; keep warm. Pour all but 1 teaspoon oil from wok. Add remaining 1 tablespoon lemon juice and remaining ingredients to wok. Stir-fry 30 seconds to heat sauce; pour over warm fish. Serve immediately.

Spicy Shrimp

Makes 3 servings
Preparation Time: 10 minutes; 3 minutes to cook

- ½ teaspoon soy sauce
- ½ teaspoon sugar
- ½ teaspoon ground coriander
- ½ cup chicken stock
- 1 pound shrimp, shelled and deveined
- 1 teaspoon dry sherry
- 1 egg white, lightly beaten
- 1½ teaspoons cornstarch
- 2 tablespoons peanut oil
- ½ teaspoon dried red pepper flakes
- ½ cup thin diagonal celery slices
- 8 Chinese dried black mushrooms, soaked in ½ cup hot water 20 minutes, drained, stems discarded, caps cut in thin strips
- 1 teaspoon cornstarch mixed with 1 teaspoon cold water

Mix first 4 ingredients; set aside. Put next 4 ingredients in bowl; toss to coat. Heat oil in wok until hot; add pepper; stir-fry 30 seconds. Add shrimp; stir-fry 1 minute. Add celery and mushrooms; stir-fry 1 minute. Add soy sauce mixture; stir-fry 30 seconds. Add cornstarch mixture; stir until slightly thickened. Serve immediately.

Steamed Bass

Makes 4 servings
Preparation Time: 10 minutes; 20 minutes to cook

- 1 sea bass *or* striped bass (about 3 pounds cleaned) with head and tail intact
- 1 tablespoon salt
- Water
- 1 tablespoon peanut oil
- 2 ¼-inch slices fresh gingerroot, peeled and minced
- 4 small cloves garlic, peeled and crushed
- 3 green onions including tops, cut in 1-inch pieces
- 2 tablespoons dry sherry
- ¼ cup soy sauce
- 1 teaspoon sesame oil

Rinse and pat fish dry; sprinkle with salt. Place fish on heatproof plate. Place plate on rack inside wok, or place fish in steamer basket. Add enough water to wok around plate or steamer basket to come within ½ inch of plate or basket. Bring water to boil. Meanwhile, heat oil in another wok until hot. Add next 4 ingredients; stir-fry 30 seconds. Add remaining ingredients; stir. Pour over fish; cover wok or put top on steamer basket. Let water boil 15 minutes or until fish is steamed to desired doneness. Serve immediately.

Fish and Seafood

Kung Pao Scallops

Makes 4 servings
Preparation Time: 50 minutes; 5 minutes to cook

- 1 pound scallops
- 1 egg white, lightly beaten
- 1 tablespoon cornstarch
- 1 tablespoon dry sherry
- 2 tablespoons soy sauce
- 1½ teaspoons hot bean sauce
- 1½ teaspoons sugar
- 1½ teaspoons vinegar
- 1 teaspoon dry sherry
- 2 cups peanut oil
- 2 teaspoons peeled and minced fresh gingerroot
- 1 clove garlic, peeled and minced
- 4 green onions including tops, thinly sliced
- 10 water chestnuts, halved
- 20 snow peas, ends and strings removed
- ½ cup unsalted roasted peanuts
- 1 teaspoon cornstarch mixed with 3 tablespoons chicken stock *or* water

Mix first 4 ingredients; set aside to marinate 30 minutes. Mix next 5 ingredients; set aside. Heat oil in wok until hot. Add scallops; stir-fry 1 minute. Remove with strainer; let drain in colander. Remove all but 1 teaspoon oil from wok. Heat oil in wok until hot. Add next 3 ingredients; stir-fry 30 seconds. Add next 3 ingredients; stir-fry 10 seconds. Add scallops with reserved soy sauce mixture; toss to combine. Stir cornstarch mixture; add to wok; stir-fry until thickened. Serve immediately.

Walnut Shrimp

Makes 4 servings
Preparation Time: 10 minutes; 7 minutes to cook

- 1 pound medium shrimp, shelled, deveined, cut in thirds
- 2 teaspoons soy sauce
- 2 teaspoons dry sherry
- ¼ teaspoon freshly ground white pepper
- 1 teaspoon cornstarch
- 3 tablespoons peanut oil
- ½ cup sliced bamboo shoots, drained
- ½ cup walnuts
- 1 ¼-inch slice fresh gingerroot, peeled
- 2 green onions including tops, sliced diagonally in 1-inch pieces
- 1 teaspoon salt
- ½ teaspoon sesame oil

Toss first 5 ingredients and 1 tablespoon oil in bowl; set aside. Heat 1 tablespoon oil in wok until hot. Add bamboo shoots and walnuts; stir-fry 1 minute; set aside. Wipe out wok with paper towels. Heat remaining 1 tablespoon oil in wok. Swirl gingerroot slice around wok 30 seconds; discard.

Add onions and shrimp mixture; stir-fry 2 minutes. Add bamboo shoots and walnuts; stir to combine. Add salt and sesame oil; stir to combine. Serve immediately.

Crab Stir-Fry with Cashews

Makes 4 servings
Preparation Time: 15 minutes; 5 minutes to cook

- 1 tablespoon cornstarch
- 1 tablespoon soy sauce
- 1 tablespoon fresh lemon juice
- ¾ cup chicken stock
- 2 tablespoons peanut oil
- ¼ pound fresh mushrooms, wiped clean and thinly sliced
- 1 6-ounce can crab meat, drained
- 4 green onions including tops, cut in thin diagonal slices
- ¼ cup sliced water chestnuts, drained
- 20 snow peas, ends and strings removed
- ⅓ cup unsalted cashews

Mix first 4 ingredients; set aside. Heat oil in wok until hot. Add mushrooms; stir-fry 1 minute. Add next 3 ingredients; stir-fry 1 minute. Add snow peas; stir-fry 1 minute. Stir cornstarch mixture; add to wok; stir-fry until slightly thickened. Add nuts; toss to combine. Serve immediately.

Fried Squid

Makes 6 servings
Preparation Time: 20 minutes; 15 to 20 minutes to cook

- 3 pounds squid
- 3 tablespoons fresh lemon juice
- 1½ teaspoons salt
- ⅛ teaspoon freshly ground white pepper
- 2 eggs, lightly beaten
- 3 tablespoons milk
- 1½ cups flour
- Peanut oil
- Lemon wedges

Cut through squid just behind eyes; squeeze out inedible beak located near cut; reserve tentacles. Feel inside body for internal shell; grasp firmly; remove from body. Rinse under cold water; peel off speckled membrane that covers body; drain body. Cut body crosswise into ½-inch rings. Cut tentacles in 1-inch pieces. Sprinkle pieces with lemon juice, salt and pepper. Mix egg and milk. Dip squid pieces in egg mixture; dredge in flour. Heat oil in wok to 350°. Fry squid pieces 3 to 5 minutes on 1 side; turn; fry 3 to 5 minutes on other side or until lightly browned. Remove using strainer; drain on paper towels. Serve immediately with lemon wedges.

Kung Pao Scallops, this page

Fish and Seafood

Sweet and Sour Salmon

Makes 4 servings
Preparation Time: 15 minutes; 40 minutes to cook

- 1½ cups water
- 1 carrot, pared and thinly sliced
- 1 tablespoon peanut oil
- 1 onion, peeled and thinly sliced
- 1 teaspoon fresh lemon juice
- 2 tablespoons sugar
- ½ cup vinegar
- 10 whole peppercorns
- 2 ribs celery, cut in 4-inch pieces
- 3 whole cloves
- 2 pounds salmon steaks, each 1-inch thick
- ⅓ to ½ cup vinegar
- 10 gingersnaps, crumbled
- ¾ cup packed light brown sugar
- ¼ cup seedless raisins
- ¼ cup dry sherry
- ¼ cup slivered almonds

Mix first 7 ingredients in wok. Tie peppercorns, celery and cloves in cheesecloth bag; add to wok. Bring to boil; reduce heat; simmer 20 minutes. Add salmon steaks; poach gently 10 minutes. Remove steaks with slotted spatula to warm serving platter; keep warm. Remove cheesecloth bag from wok. Pour enough vinegar over gingersnap crumbs to dissolve them. Add to liquid in wok with next 3 ingredients; boil 4 minutes. Add almonds; pour over fish. Serve immediately.

Sweet and Sour Shrimp

Makes 4 servings
Preparation Time: 15 minutes; 9 minutes to cook

- ½ cup flour
- 2 tablespoons cornstarch
- ½ teaspoon baking powder
- ½ teaspoon salt
- 1 egg
- 1½ cups water
- 1 cup plus 2 teaspoons peanut oil
- 16 large shrimp, shelled except for tail portion, deveined
- ½ cup catsup
- 2 tablespoons white vinegar
- 3 tablespoons sugar
- 1 large green pepper, cored, seeded and cut in 1-inch chunks
- 1 large onion, peeled, cut in eighths, separated into pieces
- 1 15½-ounce can pineapple chunks, drained
- 2 teaspoons cornstarch mixed with 2 teaspoons cold water

Mix flour, cornstarch, baking powder, salt, egg, ½ cup water and 1 teaspoon oil in bowl until smooth; set aside. Heat 1 cup oil in wok until hot. Holding shrimp by tail, dip one at a time into batter, letting excess drip back into bowl. Slide shrimp into hot oil; fry until golden brown, 1 to 2 minutes each. Fry two or three at a time. Drain on paper towels. Pour out all oil except 1 tablespoon. Add remaining 1 cup water, 1 teaspoon oil, catsup, vinegar and sugar to wok; bring to boil. Add green pepper and onion; return to boil. Stir-fry 2 minutes. Add pineapple; return to boil. Stir cornstarch mixture; add to wok; stir to thicken. Add shrimp; stir gently until heated through. Serve immediately.

Shrimp and Lobster Stir-Fry

Makes 6 servings
Preparation Time: 20 minutes; 8½ minutes to cook

- 2 tablespoons peanut oil
- 2 cloves garlic, peeled and finely chopped
- 2 ¼-inch slices fresh gingerroot, peeled and minced
- 3 green onions including tops, thinly sliced
- 1 8-ounce can sliced water chestnuts, drained
- 1 8-ounce can sliced bamboo shoots, drained
- ¼ pound fresh mushrooms, wiped clean, thinly sliced
- ¾ pound large shrimp, shelled except for tail, deveined and patted dry
- ¾ pound lobster tails, thin undershells cut away, meat and shells cut crosswise in segments
- ⅓ pound snow peas, ends and strings removed
- 1½ cups chicken stock
- 2 tablespoons cornstarch
- 2 tablespoons soy sauce
- 1 teaspoon salt
- 1 teaspoon sugar
- ¼ teaspoon freshly ground white pepper

Heat oil in wok until hot. Add next 3 ingredients; stir-fry 1 minute. Add next 3 ingredients; stir-fry 2 minutes. Add next 3 ingredients; stir-fry 2 minutes. Add ¾ cup chicken stock; cover; cook 1 minute. Mix remaining ¾ cup chicken stock with remaining ingredients; add to wok; stir-fry until slightly thickened, about 30 seconds. Cover; cook 1 minute. Serve immediately.

Note: Shell is left on tail of shrimp and on lobster segments because it adds flavor. Meat of both shellfish can be removed easily with fork. Use the lobster meat in body, legs and claws for salads.

International Dishes

Brandied Beef

Makes 6 servings
Preparation Time: 1 hour, 45 minutes

- 1 teaspoon salt
- 1 teaspoon paprika
- ½ teaspoon dried basil
- ¼ teaspoon dried thyme
- 2 tablespoons flour
- 2 pounds beef stew meat
- 2 tablespoons peanut oil
- 1 clove garlic, peeled and crushed
- 1 large onion, peeled and cut in 8 wedges
- ½ cup beef stock
- ½ cup brandy
- 2 cups fresh mushrooms, wiped clean and halved if large
  Hot buttered cooked egg noodles

Mix first 5 ingredients. Lightly dredge meat in flour mixture. Heat oil in wok until hot. Brown meat in batches, removing to plate. Add garlic and onion; stir-fry 30 seconds. Return meat to wok with stock and brandy. Reduce heat to medium; cover; simmer 1 hour. Add mushrooms; stir; cook 10 minutes, covered. Serve immediately with buttered egg noodles.

Chicken Cacciatore

Makes 6 servings
Preparation Time: 1 hour, 30 minutes

- ¼ cup peanut oil
- 2 chickens, cut into serving pieces and patted dry
- 2 onions, peeled and chopped
- 1 green pepper, cored, seeded and chopped
- 1 red pepper, cored, seeded and chopped
- 3 cloves garlic, peeled and crushed
- 1½ cups tomato puree
- ¼ cup dry red wine
- 1½ teaspoons salt
- ¼ teaspoon freshly ground black pepper
- ¼ teaspoon ground allspice
- 3 tablespoons tomato paste
- 1 teaspoon dried oregano
- 1 teaspoon dried basil
  Hot cooked spinach noodles

Heat oil in wok until hot. Brown chicken pieces on both sides, a few at a time; place on plate. Add onions, peppers and garlic; stir-fry 2 minutes. Add remaining ingredients except chicken and noodles; bring to boil; simmer 10 minutes. Return chicken to wok; simmer, covered, 15 to 20 minutes. Uncover; simmer 10 minutes. Serve immediately with spinach noodles.

Portuguese Codfish

Makes 4 servings
Preparation Time: 1 hour; overnight to soak fish

- 1 pound dried codfish, soaked overnight in cold water, drained
  Water
- 3 potatoes
- ¼ cup peanut oil
- 2 large onions, peeled and sliced
- 1 clove garlic, peeled and crushed
- ¼ cup finely chopped ripe olives
- ½ teaspoon dried dillweed
- ⅓ cup dry vermouth
  Freshly ground black pepper to taste
  Fresh parsley, chopped

Place fish in wok; cover with cold water; bring to boil; boil 20 minutes or until fish is opaque. Remove; set aside to cool; remove skin and bones if necessary. Cook potatoes in same water in wok until tender; remove; discard water. Peel and slice potatoes; set aside. Heat oil in clean wok; add onions; stir-fry until limp but not brown. Add fish, potatoes and next 5 ingredients. Gently stir-fry 3 minutes. Cover; cook on low heat 10 to 15 minutes. Garnish with parsley. Serve immediately.

Veal and Mushrooms

Makes 4 to 6 servings
Preparation Time: 1¼ hours

- 2 tablespoons peanut oil
- 2 pounds lean veal, cut in 1½-inch cubes
- ¾ pound fresh mushrooms, sliced
- 2 tablespoons flour
- 1½ cups chicken stock
  Salt and freshly ground black pepper to taste
- ⅓ cup dry vermouth
- 2 tablespoons chopped fresh parsley
  Hot cooked rice or noodles

Heat oil in wok until hot. Sear veal cubes in batches over medium heat; do not crowd; remove to bowl. Return veal to wok with mushrooms; stir-fry 3 minutes. Sprinkle with flour; toss to combine. Reduce heat; add stock and salt and pepper; mix well. Cover; simmer 50 minutes or until meat is tender. Add vermouth; toss. Sprinkle with parsley. Serve immediately on rice.

Ratatouille

Makes 6 servings
Preparation Time: 30 minutes; 10 to 12 minutes to cook

- 1 unpeeled large eggplant, cubed
- 2 tablespoons olive oil
- 3 tomatoes, cored, peeled, seeded and chopped
- 3 unpeeled zucchini, thinly sliced
- 2 onions, peeled and diced
- 1 clove garlic, peeled and crushed
- 2 tablespoons chopped fresh parsley

Place eggplant cubes in colander; sprinkle generously with salt. Let stand 30 minutes; rinse under cold running water; spread out cubes on towel and pat dry. Heat oil in wok until hot. Add all ingredients except parsley; stir-fry until vegetables are soft but not browned. Stir in parsley. Serve immediately.

Continental Calves' Liver

Makes 4 servings
Preparation Time: 20 minutes

- 1 pound calves' liver, skinned, sliced 1½-inch-thick and cut in 1-inch pieces
  Salt and freshly ground black pepper to taste
- ¼ cup flour
- ¼ cup peanut oil
- 2 medium onions, peeled and thinly sliced
- ½ cup dry vermouth
- 2 tablespoons tomato puree
- 2 tablespoons chopped fresh parsley

Sprinkle liver with salt and pepper; lightly dredge in flour. Heat oil in wok until hot. Add onion; stir-fry until limp but not brown. Increase heat; add liver; stir-fry 3 to 4 minutes. Drain off excess oil from wok. Add vermouth and puree; toss to mix. Cook 2 to 3 minutes. Sprinkle with parsley; serve immediately.

Italian Shrimp and Vegetables

Makes 4 servings
Preparation Time: 15 minutes; 10 minutes to cook

- 2 tablespoons peanut oil
- 1 pound large shrimp, shelled and deveined
- 1 pound unpeeled zucchini, thinly sliced
- 1 large onion, peeled and thinly sliced
- 2 cloves garlic, peeled and crushed
- ¼ cup minced fresh parsley
- 1 teaspoon salt
- ¼ teaspoon freshly ground black pepper
- 1½ teaspoons fresh lemon juice
- ¼ cup freshly grated Parmesan cheese

Heat oil in wok until hot. Add shrimp; stir-fry 3

minutes or until pink; remove with strainer. Add zucchini, onion and garlic; stir-fry until tender-crisp. Add next 3 ingredients and shrimp. Cover; simmer 2 minutes. Uncover; sprinkle with lemon juice and cheese. Toss to combine thoroughly. Serve immediately.

Favorite Chili

Makes 4 servings
Preparation Time: 5 minutes; 2 to 3 hours to cook

- 1 pound coarsely ground lean beef
- 1 large clove garlic, peeled and crushed
- 2 tablespoons flour
- 1 teaspoon ground cumin
- 1 to 2 tablespoons chili powder
- ½ teaspoon salt
- ¼ teaspoon freshly ground black pepper
- 1½ cups vegetable cocktail juice
- ½ teaspoon Worcestershire sauce
- 1 15-ounce can red kidney beans, drained, optional

Stir-fry meat and garlic in wok over medium heat until meat is browned and crumbled. Add flour; stir to blend. Add next 6 ingredients; bring to boil. Reduce heat to low; cover; cook 2 to 3 hours, stirring occasionally. Mixture should not cook dry; reduce heat and add more vegetable juice if needed. Add beans 1 hour before end of cooking time, if desired. Serve immediately.

Note: This freezes well.

Greek Lamb Stew

Makes 6 servings
Preparation Time: 20 minutes; 1½ hours to cook

- 2 tablespoons peanut oil
- 2 pounds boned, cubed lean lamb
  Salt and freshly ground black pepper to taste
- 3 small onions, peeled and chopped
- 2 ribs celery, chopped
- 3 carrots, pared and thinly sliced
- 2 small cloves garlic, peeled and crushed
- 2 cups water
- 4 eggs, separated
- ¼ cup fresh lemon juice

Heat oil in wok until hot. Brown meat in batches; season with salt and pepper. Reduce heat; add onion; stir-fry until translucent. Return meat to wok with next 4 ingredients; simmer, covered, 1 hour or until meat is tender. Add more water if needed. Remove from heat; skim off any fat. Beat egg whites until they hold peaks; gradually beat in yolks. Slowly add lemon juice, beating constantly. Pour over stew; stir to combine and heat thoroughly. Serve immediately.

Favorite Chili, this page

Desserts

Custard with Oriental Sauce

Makes 6 servings
Preparation Time: 10 minutes; 30 to 40 minutes to bake; 3 to 4 hours to chill

   3 eggs
   3 tablespoons sugar
  ⅛ teaspoon salt
  ¼ teaspoon almond extract
  ½ teaspoon vanilla extract
2¼ cups scalded milk
    Oriental Fruit

Preheat oven to 350°. Beat eggs, sugar, salt, almond and vanilla extracts together in bowl. Gradually add milk, stirring constantly. Divide equally among 6 custard cups. Place cups in large shallow pan; fill pan with boiling water that reaches to level of custard in cups. Bake 30 to 40 minutes or until knife inserted in center of custard comes out clean. Cool at room temperature 10 minutes; cover; chill thoroughly. Prepare Oriental Fruit. To serve, run knife around outside edges of custards; invert onto serving dishes; top with Oriental Fruit.

Oriental Fruit

 ⅓ cup sugar
 1 tablespoon cornstarch
 1 cup fresh orange juice
 1 11-ounce can mandarin orange segments, drained
 1 11-ounce can litchi nuts, drained

Stir sugar and cornstarch together in 2-quart saucepan. Place over low heat; gradually add orange juice, stirring constantly. Bring to boil, stirring constantly until thickened. Remove from heat; stir in orange segments and nuts. Cover and chill.

Fresh Pineapple with Grand Marnier

Makes 4 servings
Preparation Time: 15 minutes

 1 large pineapple
¼ cup Grand Marnier

Cut pineapple in half lengthwise through top crown. Cut halves lengthwise, making 4 wedges. With sharp knife, cut out core that runs length of each wedge. Cut pineapple from shell in 1 piece; cut into bite-size pieces; pile back onto shell. Repeat with remaining pineapple wedges. Pour 1 tablespoon Grand Marnier over each serving; serve immediately.

Note: Pineapple can be cut, wrapped in plastic wrap and refrigerated 4 to 6 hours in advance; pour on Grand Marnier just before serving.

Fortune Cookies

Makes 48
Preparation Time: 15 minutes; 10 minutes to bake

  5 to 6 egg whites (¾ cup)
1⅔ cups sugar
  ¼ teaspoon salt
  1 cup unsalted butter, melted
  1 cup flour
  ¾ cup very finely chopped blanched almonds
  ½ teaspoon vanilla
 48 fortunes written on 3 x ¾-inch strips of paper

Preheat oven to 350°. Mix first 3 ingredients in bowl until sugar dissolves. Stir in remaining ingredients, one at a time, until well blended. Drop dough by level teaspoonfuls onto ungreased baking sheet; allow 6 cookies per sheet, spacing well apart. Bake 10 minutes or until edges are golden brown. Remove cookies, one at a time, from baking sheet. Place 1 fortune in center of each cookie; fold cookie in half; pinch sides together. Work quickly before cookies cool and harden.

Almond Custard with Mandarin Oranges

Makes 6 to 9 servings
Preparation Time: 10 minutes; overnight to chill

 2 cups water
 1 stick (about ¼ ounce) agar-agar, cut in small pieces
 1 cup evaporated milk
⅓ cup sugar
 1 tablespoon almond extract
 1 11-ounce can mandarin orange segments, drained

Bring 1 cup water to boil in saucepan; add agar-agar; stir until dissolved, about 3 minutes. Add milk and sugar; return to boil. Boil 1 minute, stirring constantly. Add extract and remaining 1 cup hot water. Cook, stirring constantly, until mixture returns to boil. Strain into 9-inch square glass pan. Cool at room temperature; cover with plastic wrap; refrigerate overnight to set. To serve, cut into 1-inch cubes; divide among 6 to 9 bowls; top with orange segments. Serve immediately.

Hong Kong Sundae

Makes enough sauce for 6 to 8 servings
Preparation Time: 10 minutes; 3 to 4 hours to chill

    1 8½-ounce can crushed pineapple with juice
    2 tablespoons cornstarch
    1 11-ounce can mandarin orange segments with
       liquid
    6 to 8 preserved kumquats, drained and chopped
    2 tablespoons chopped preserved ginger
       Vanilla ice cream

Mix 2 tablespoons of the pineapple juice with cornstarch; set aside. Place pineapple and remaining juice, orange segments and liquid, kumquats and ginger in top of double boiler over medium heat. Heat to just below boiling. Stir cornstarch mixture; add to double boiler. Stir until thickened. Pour into bowl; refrigerate until completely cold. Serve as sauce over ice cream.

Note: This sauce can be made several days in advance.

Melon Balls in Liqueur

Makes 3 servings
Preparation Time: 30 minutes plus chilling time

    ½ cup watermelon balls, seeds removed
    ½ cup honeydew melon balls
    ½ cup cantaloupe melon balls
    3 tablespoons melon-flavored liqueur

Mix melon balls gently in glass bowl; chill thoroughly. To serve, divide melon balls equally among 3 glass serving bowls; drizzle 1 tablespoon liqueur over each bowl. Serve immediately.

Red Wine Oranges

Makes 6 servings
Preparation Time: 10 minutes; 3 to 4 hours to chill

    ¾ cup sugar
    1 cup water
    1 cup dry red wine
    5 whole cloves
    2 cinnamon sticks
    4 strips lemon peel
    6 large naval oranges, peeled and sectioned

Mix first 6 ingredients in wok; bring to boil. Lower heat; simmer 10 minutes to make light syrup. Strain to remove cloves, cinnamon sticks and lemon peel. Pour over oranges in bowl; refrigerate until completely chilled.

Almond Cookies

Makes 4 dozen
Preparation Time: 15 minutes; 20 minutes to bake

    1 cup sugar
    1⅓ cups shortening
    1 egg
    1 teaspoon almond extract
    3 cups flour
    1 teaspoon baking soda
    ½ teaspoon salt
    48 blanched whole almonds

Preheat oven to 350°. Cream butter and shortening until fluffy. Add egg and almond extract; beat 1 minute. Sift flour, baking soda and salt together; add to creamed mixture gradually, beating constantly. Roll dough into 1-inch balls; place 1 inch apart on greased baking sheet. Press center of each ball down gently; fill depression with 1 almond. Bake 20 minutes. Remove to wire rack to cool.

Note: Cookies can be frozen.

Fruit Stir-Fry

Makes 4 servings
Preparation Time: 15 minutes; 10 to 15 minutes to cook

    2 firm pears (preferably Bosc), peeled, cored and cut
       in crosswise slices
    3 cups semidry white wine (such as Riesling)
       Pinch salt
    12 strawberries, hulled and cut in crosswise slices
    2 ripe mangoes, peeled and sectioned
    1 kiwi fruit, peeled and sliced
    3 tablespoons unsalted butter
    1 pint raspberries, rinsed gently

Combine pears, wine and salt in wok; simmer 2 to 3 minutes or until pears are just tender. Add strawberries; simmer 1 minute. Add mangoes; simmer 1 minute. Add kiwi fruit; simmer 1 minute. Fruit should be tender, but not falling apart. Carefully remove fruit with strainer; keep warm. Boil liquid in wok over highest heat to reduce by one-half. Lower heat; swirl in butter. Return cooked fruit to sauce. Add raspberries; mix gently just until raspberries are warmed through. Remove fruit to individual bowls using strainer; boil sauce further if it seems too thin. Spoon sauce over fruit.

Note: This makes a luscious sauce for vanilla ice cream.

Bamboo Shoots Young shoots of tropical bamboo. Sold whole or sliced in cans. After opening, rinse in cold water. Store in water in refrigerator up to 1 week. Change water every 2 days.

Bean Curd Also known as tofu. A nutritious, low-calorie source of protein. Made of pressed pureed soybeans formed into cakes. It is white and has the consistency of firm custard. Bland in taste, it absorbs the flavor of other ingredients. Can be fried, simmered, baked, steamed, or used in stir-frying. Store in water in refrigerator up to 1 week. Change water daily.

Bean Sauce* Made of soybeans, flour, salt and water. Hot bean sauce is a more spicy version used in Szechwan dishes. After opening, refrigerate in tightly covered jar. Keeps indefinitely.

Bean Sprouts Tiny sprouts that are white, sweet, plump and crunchy. Fresh sprouts are preferable to canned sprouts. Rinse in cold water before using. Store in water in refrigerator up to 1 week. Change water daily.

Black Beans* Salted and fermented, these beans season fish and meat dishes. Store in tightly covered container indefinitely.

Bok Choy Green vegetable with long white stalks and ruffled leaves. Store in plastic wrap in refrigerator up to 1 week.

Cellophane Noodles* Also known as bean thread or vermicelli. Made of mung bean flour and look as if they are made from cellophane. Must be presoaked if used in soups; not necessary to presoak for deep-frying. Keep indefinitely.

Chicken Stock Interchangeable with canned chicken broth although homemade chicken stock is preferable.

Dried Orange or Tangerine Peel* Used for flavoring meat and poultry. Keeps indefinitely.

Dried Red Pepper Flakes* Made from dried orange or red hot peppers. Include seed which are essential for hotness. Keep indefinitely.

Ears of Baby Corn Tiny ears of corn, 2 to 3 inches long, sold in cans. Store in liquid in covered can in refrigerator up to 6 days.

Egg Roll Skins Squares of egg noodle dough in which to place filling. Store in refrigerator up to 5 days. May be frozen.

Five-Spice Powder* Combination of 5 ground spices—cinnamon, fennel, star anise, cloves and Szechwan peppercorns. Used for stewing and barbecuing meats. Reddish brown in color. Keeps indefinitely.

Garlic Do not substitute garlic powder. Never burn garlic while cooking, or it will impart bitter taste. Store in dry place.

Ginger, preserved* Used in sweet and sour dishes for color and flavoring. Store in tightly covered jar in refrigerator. Keeps indefinitely.

Gingerroot, fresh Very important seasoning in stir-fry cooking. There is no substitute. Sold by the piece or by weight, fresh gingerroot is knobby in appearance. Always peel before using. Wrap in plastic; keep at room temperature 2 to 3 weeks. Never refrigerate. Can be peeled, sliced and frozen; do not thaw before using.

Green Onion Also called scallion. Long, thin onion with white and green part.

Hoisin Sauce* Spicy reddish-brown sauce with creamy consistency, made of Chinese pumpkin, sugar, spices and soy sauce. After opening, store in covered jar several weeks.

Lychee* Subtropical fruit. Delicious in sweet and sour sauce. Used in desserts. Store in tightly covered jar in refrigerator several days.

Mushrooms, Chinese Dried Black* Rinse and soak in hot water 20 minutes before using. Use caps, discard tough stems. Keep indefinitely.

Mushrooms, Cloud Ear* Also known as tree ears or fungus mushrooms. Black and crinkled, they expand two to three times their dried size when soaked. Soft in texture, subtle in taste. Must be soaked in hot water before using. Cook with vegetables, chicken, meat or soup.

Mushrooms, Straw* Delicious with crab meat. After opening, refrigerate, covered with water, in jar. Change water every 2 days. Keep several weeks.

Mustard, Chinese Used for dipping sauce. Make in small amounts; mix powdered or dry mustard with cold water and allow to mellow 30 minutes to remove harsh, bitter taste. Hot and pungent. Keeps indefinitely.

Oyster Sauce* Thick Cantonese sauce made from oyster extract, but has no fishy taste or odor. Adds flavor to meat, poultry and noodles. Store covered in refrigerator

Peanut Oil Preferred for stir-frying. Can be reused if strained and refrigerated. Discard when dark and full of residue. Oil for cooking fish should be kept separate and reused only for fish. Refrigerate after use.

Plum Sauce* Made of plums, ginger, apricots, chilies, vinegar, sugar and water. Used as condiment. Store in covered container in refrigerator a few months.

Rice, glutinous* Also known as sweet rice. Round grains that become soft and sticky when cooked. Used for making dumplings, sweet dishes and poultry stuffing.

Rice Sticks Also called rice noodles. White, thin, fragile and slightly wavy, these sticks are made from ground rice. Used deep-fried and in soups. Store on shelf indefinitely.

Sesame Seed Oil* Reddish brown, made from roasted sesame seed. Generally used as seasoning; the thicker the oil, the better the flavor. Keeps indefinitely.

Snow Peas Also known as pea pods. Flat, light green, crisp and sweet. Always select thin snow peas. Avoid frozen pea pods because they give up too much moisture in stir-fried dishes. Remove ends and strings. Slice through stem end, but do not sever string. Pull stem end and attached string down pod. Repeat on opposite end for other string. Usually left whole for cooking and eating. Store in refrigerator 1 to 3 days.

Soy Sauce One of the most important seasonings in stir-fry cookery. There are two kinds. Thin soy sauce has a clear brown color and a beanlike aroma. Use it for delicate dishes. Dark soy sauce is very dark in color, has a sheen and is slightly thicker than light soy sauce. Dark soy sauce is slightly sweet and the bean aroma is muted. Store on shelf indefinitely.

Star Anise* Reddish-brown Chinese spice resembling 8-pointed star. Smells like licorice. Flavors meat and poultry. Store in covered jar indefinitely.

Tofu See bean curd.

Water Chestnuts Used as vegetable with meat and poultry. Delicious with snow peas. Sold whole or sliced in cans. After opening, cover with water and refrigerate. Change water twice a week. Keeps several weeks.

Wine, Chinese Rice wine fortified to the strength of sherry. Use dry sherry as substitute, but never cooking sherry.

Won Ton Skins Small squares or rounds of egg noodle dough in which fillings are placed. Sold in 1-pound packages. Keep refrigerated 1 week. Can be frozen.

*denotes items found in Oriental and/or specialty food stores

Clockwise, from top:
Almond Cookies, page 61
Fruit Stir-Fry, page 61
Melon Balls in Liqueur, page 61

Index

C
D
E
F
G
H
I
J
K
L

5
6
7
8
9
0
1